KU-049-901

CLASSIC
HAULIERS

CLASSIC HAULIERS

Bob Tuck

The Fitzjames Press

THE FITZJAMES PRESS
an imprint of
Motor Racing Publications Ltd
Unit 6, The Pilton Estate, 46 Pitlake,
Croydon, CR0 3RY, England.

First published 1989

Copyright © 1989 Bob Tuck and The Fitzjames Press

All rights reserved. No part of this publication may be reproduced, stored in a retrieval system, or transmitted, in any form or by any means, electronic, mechanical, photocopying, recording or otherwise, without the prior permission of The Fitzjames Press.

British Library Cataloguing in Publication Data
Tuck, Bob
    Classic hauliers.
    1. Great Britain. Road freight transport services, history
    I. Title
    388.3'24'0941

    ISBN 0 948358 02 5

Photosetting by Tek-Art Ltd, West Wickham, Kent.
Printed in Great Britain by The Amadeus Press Ltd, Huddersfield, West Yorkshire.

Front cover:

Since the late 1970s, a striking feature of Suttons' livery has been the Union Flag motif across the cab front, symbolizing the company's pride in being British, and also its pride in using British-built trucks. ERFs now form the lion's share of the fleet and, from a very modest start, tankers account for about half of the total of more than 200 road-going vehicles. Suttons' principal road tanker depots are situated at Whitley, near Warrington, at Billingham and at Oldbury, Birmingham. There is also a depot at Longtown, near Carlisle, and the company undertakes responsibility for an area in the tanker industry's Emergency Load Transfer Scheme. Suttons' tankers convey a wide variety of liquid products, a notable example being the bulk movement of beer. The C-type ERF 2+3 38-tonner shown here is on chemical carriage work, the general purpose tank being equipped for air-pressure discharge.

Back cover:

The resplendent fleet of the Edinburgh-based operator, Pollocks, has long been admired by both transport enthusiasts and rival haulage contractors alike. Pictured here in the company's old premises at 101 Newbigging, Musselburgh, 'Gemini II' is a particularly fine example of the Atkinson eight-wheelers that were used by Pollocks from the early 1960s. This Geoff Milne photograph dates from July 1971, when Pollocks were about to sell out to the Hilton empire, only to buy the fleet back four years later when Hiltons went into receivership. The Atkinson carries the Kerr tartan, whilst the four-wheeled Albion with Ergomatic cab in the background, entitled 'Star Trek', has Erskine tartan. Using names from sources like spacecraft and television programmes for the fleet's vehicles is a tradition that was started by Ian Pollock and continues to this day.

Contents

Introduction

I must confess that I have always tended to respond more readily to a vehicle painted up in a famous fleet owner's colours than to a drably anonymous one. The names of the carriers involved are richly evocative in themselves, each with its fund of memories and associations, each with a different story to be told, and even though the truck itself may be like many others, it is that livery and ownership which makes all the difference. So writing a book on Classic Hauliers allows a degree of personal indulgence in making the choice of what inevitably has to be a limited selection. The main criteria that I have adopted for each company to merit inclusion is that they have all been involved in road transport for a lengthy period and that they all in different ways have something rather special about them.

Whilst endeavouring to give as wide a geographical spread to the contents as possible, I have also tried to reflect both the variation in size among the organizations and the diversity of tasks carried out by the people who ensure that the life blood of this country's trade can be transported to every part that needs it.

Fleet lists

To give an extra dimension to the picture of the many-sided business of road transport, fleet lists are included for most of the operators described. The one obvious drawback to providing a list is that, in the case of an active company, it will inevitably very quickly be out of date. With many hauliers adopting a policy of renewing all their vehicles over a five-year period, it may well be that in a fleet numbering more than 200 vehicles, 40 or 50 old ones will be replaced by new in the space of a year. Partly for that reason, no lists are included for either Suttons or Autocar & Transporters. Robsons Distribution operate a similarly large fleet but have long made a point of updating their followers with regular lists: even there, though, the list prepared in the first half of 1989 will soon be overtaken by changes. So what is published here should be taken as a representative indication of each fleet's make-up rather than an exact record.

The lists for the hauliers of yesteryear have been put together from personal recollection and observation, more precise records being no longer available. Again, I hope they will provide a guide at least, though I am sure more vehicles than listed were used by all these operations.

Much of the excitement for spotters, of course, lies in finding vehicles not mentioned in the lists or, even better, finding mistakes in the lists that only the spotter is aware of!

Acknowledgements

A book of this nature could not have been written were it not for the time and co-operation that I was afforded by all the companies involved but beyond that general debt of gratitude I think it would be remiss of me should I not specifically mention some of the many people who have been particularly helpful: Norman Byrne, Siddle and George Cook, Roger Cullimore, Lou and Joe Elliot, Bob Exley, Tommy and Jimmy Gibb, Archie and Ken Glendinning, Gary Hutchinson, Tony Knowles, Alastair Laird, Rodney Kneale, Kevin O'Brien, Norman Parker, Ian and Scott Pollock, Albert Robson, John and David Silbermann, Ken Simmons, Michael Sutton, Eddie Tomlinson, George 'Jock' Walker, Catherine Williams.

To Peter White I must express thanks for finding them and to Frank Richardson thanks for the use of some excellent Pollock photographs. To George Baker and Howard Nunnick I must once again offer thanks for the time they have spent in finding out information that makes my captions far more interesting.

Never forgetting my wife Sylvia who continues to give help, guidance and the occasional kick of encouragement, I feel the real stalwart in the compilation of this book must be Geoff Milne. Someone I am pleased to call a friend, Geoff has probably forgotten more than I will ever know about Classic Hauliers; though he will probably be embarrassed when he reads this, were it not for his inspiration and unselfishness I doubt if this book would ever have been written.

Bob Tuck

About 1965, Stan Robson acquired XL 453 just to show the people of Carlisle what had started him off in transport forty years earlier. Believed to have been bought at a sale in Kilmarnock, the Model T Ford was not one of the vehicles that was sold on to United Glass and it has been kept both in the ownership of the Robson family and in regular use. Even though the following 'Border Symbol' can carry close to 20 times as much payload as the Ford, the S34 Foden – the first of that marque to have the tilting cab – is a far easier vehicle to drive. The Ford may have three pedals on the floor, but the accelerator isn't one of them, it's a lever instead: to engage bottom gear the left-hand pedal has to be pressed and held down. For reverse, the centre pedal is held down as long as it is required for the vehicle to go backwards. That leaves the right-hand pedal to operate a transmission brake.

1: Robsons Distribution Services

To start off a book on Classic Hauliers, I make no apologies for selecting Robsons Border Transport Ltd. This is not the company name currently in use: instead, to project the image of a national transport concern, the title Robsons Distribution Services has been adopted and marketed vigorously by the haulier's current owners, the Bunzl Group.

To those who ask, 'What's in a name?' many will reply that where pride and reputation are concerned, everything is in the name. It was probably Stan Robson's idea of naming his vehicles individually that has helped to make his fleet so memorable. Now counted in hundreds, every truck has a name, each name beginning with 'Border', an unashamed announcement that Carlisle and the Border country of England and Scotland is where the heart of Robsons lies, where the company was born and has flourished.

It was in 1936 that Stan Robson hit upon the notion of proudly naming his first new Foden 'Border Queen'. By then Robson had already put eleven hard years of carrying experience behind him: in hindsight, 1925 probably had not been the best time for a 19-year-old to set up a new transport concern! The general strike came in 1926 and the world depression of the early 1930s spread even to Cumberland.

Stan was born and bred in the village of Hethersgill, in the heart of 'God's country', equidistant from Carlisle, Brampton and Longtown. When he moved into Carlisle in search of more carting traffic, the tool of the trade that he adopted was a weathered Ford Model T. Keeping it going on the road during the day meant that many nights were spent with some part of the engine on the family kitchen table receiving painstaking attention. Even Stan's wife Kathleen became very adept at the regular task of grinding the valves in.

By 1933 the mantle of Robson flagship had been taken by a three-ton Bedford. With it had come Stan's younger brother, Albert, who was set to work as a driver as soon as he was old enough to get a driving licence. Stan was never a man who enjoyed exceptionally good health, but the working routine demanded from both Albert and the Bedford was one only the fittest could endure. A good contract was won to service the local farms with cattle feed, and initially this saw the Bedford run empty down to Selby and the British Oil Cake Mills. A tie-up with a rag and bone merchant in Carlisle soon cut down on this empty running, as, hauling the maximum he could squeeze on, Albert ran south to Batley loaded up with rags and waste woollens. This part of the journey was easy, but later, running into the border farms with sacked feed, the canny farmers would only accept delivery once those heavy sacks were lifted up rickety flights of stairs into the storage loft.

This sole Bedford and driver was run on what was called a 'catnap' basis, perhaps best illustrated by what an AA motorcycle patrolman said to Albert when he was talking to him at Scotch Corner one day. 'Robson must have a lot of these Bedfords,' the Automobile Association man said. 'How's that?' asked the young Robson. 'Well, whenever I'm out I always see one working on the A66.'

The hard work paid off and by 1936 Stan decided to commit himself to something far bigger than the Fords or Bedford and, more importantly, something brand new. Very few people were interested in talking to the man from up north with virtually no fleet and little money to mention, but in William Foden, Stan Robson found someone who *would* listen to the Carlisle man's hopes and someone who extended the hand of trust towards him. So a bond was formed which, over the following 40 years, saw many more Fodens pass into Robson ownership.

The new Foden was bought 'on the knock' as the terminology of the day described the transaction but it was one of Stan Robson's proudest moments. A gleaming new 'Chinese Six' capable of carrying 10 or even 12 tons of

Not the original 'Border Queen', but this 1948 S18 four-wheeler is believed to be only the second Foden to carry the very first of the Robson fleet's celebrated 'Border' names. Seen in this old photo leaving the premises of Border Dairy at Carlisle, the rigid is en route for the Co-operative Wholesale Society creamery at Stocksfield, Northumberland, a regular destination for Carlisle milk. Stan first saw 'Border Queen' painted on a charabanc owned by his future father-in-law and thought the name had a grand ring to it.

Purists might say that 'Border Samson' was a totally defiled version of the original 1953 S18 'Border Courier'. In fact, at the time of writing Robert Chicken is in the process of restoring the vehicle to its original eight-wheeled dropsider condition. However those of the Robson staff who worked the eight-legger in its crane form were regularly surprised what the old rig was capable of. The original wheelbase had been shortened about five feet. The crane superstructure is believed to have started life as the main part of a four-wheeled crane which was registered HAO 79 and named 'Border Goliath'. This Geoff Milne photograph was taken in Carlisle about 1973.

10

payload, perhaps three or four times what the little Bedford had carried, the vehicle was his Queen and he wanted everyone to know it. The two-tone red Foden soon had its name 'Border Queen' proudly emblazoned across the front, and the Robson trademark was forged.

Sid Robson, another brother of Stan's, was the Queen's first driver and he too was proud of what he was driving. It was only a five-cylinder Gardner engine but he reported that all the horsepower was alive and kicking and, as far as fuel consumption was concerned, it was remarkably frugal – not surprising as the Gardner engine was already known for being able almost to 'run on fresh air'. The three-axle configuration with two at the front meant that there were four wheels to turn with no power steering so Sid's arms soon had to be strong, and the hydraulic booster brakes required lots of driver strength as well. But the Queen was something special and she was soon to pay her debts off.

By 1938, Stan felt ready to commit himself to an even more worrying time when Thistle Transport came up for disposal. Although Carlisle based, the company was owned by Alexander Smart of Leith and, naturally, other Scottish firms looked keenly at this going concern. Carlisle may seem an obscure location for a transport centre, but as later BRS operations were to show, virtually all Scottish-bound traffic ran up the A6 and through the town. The A1 up the east coast may have been called 'The Great North Road' but the A6 was the really important route and even the daunting Shap and Beattock summits didn't prevent this west coast preference. So Carlisle was an ideal staging post or changeover point for long distance men. Carlisle was also Stan Robson's home town and he had a dream to make its

haulage needs all his own. The first step along that path was buying out the vehicles and more especially the licences of Thistle as the Robson plan was put into operation.

Thistle ran a mixed fleet of about 15 vehicles although they too favoured Fodens. Repainted two-tone Robson red, they were soon also adorned with names, best remembered being BHH 516, 'Border Majestic', a 6x4 Foden flat which ran with a four-wheeled Dyson drawbar trailer. No ball-bearing turntables on this 'dangler' – the steering axle had a steel-on-steel pivot which meant that turning the trailer wheels by hand was almost an impossibility. Another vehicle from the Thistle stable drivers recall was a Reo four-wheeler which due to its natural turn of speed was named 'Border Flyer'.

At this time, Robsons were a true general haulier. With vehicles like Bedford BHH 440 they moved household loads of furniture inside the Luton van body whilst Albion Chieftans like 'Border Lassie' were found to be ideal for milk churn collection as they had a far longer, 22ft body and were a lot closer to the ground than the stronger Fodens. If Stan Robson was to worry about finding extra traffic for his expanding fleet, the question was answered with the arrival of hostilities and the commandeering of the wagons under Government control. During the war, Robsons fleet went far and wide. Ships' propellors to Northern Ireland, foodstuffs and munitions on the mainland, even assistance with the nightly evacuation of people from Liverpool were normal tasks as part of the war effort.

With the return of peace, Stan Robson set out to expand his haulage empire further, buying new Fodens whenever he could afford them, although not every example was as

Stan Robson had his own particular likes and dislikes among the different types of Foden cab that were produced. He never bought any of the first glassfibre cabs (S21s – known as 'Mickey Mouses') but hung on buying the last of the coachbuilt S20 ones until the first S34 tilt-cabs were introduced. 'Border Eagle' was also very much a one-off because it was the only S40-cabbed vehicle run by Robsons. Being aptly named after its Rolls-Royce Mark 3 220bhp Eagle diesel engine, the tractor was the pride and joy of driver Geordie Graham who lived at Longtown. Stan Robson let few of his men play around with his vehicles by adding wheel embellishers and the like, but the pride which Graham had in his outfit was why he was one of the exceptions. This Geoff Milne photograph was taken in Carlisle about 1973.

Seddon Atkinson have never figured strongly in the Robson fleet although about six 401 tractive units came into service during 1981–82. 'Border Envoy', with chassis number 74284 and fitted with the Rolls-Royce 265 engine, is pictured at its normal operating base at The Bridge of Allan. On a dedicated contract for United Closures & Plastics – now part of the Metal Box Group – the artic ran between the factory and a store at Grangemouth. The step-frame semi-trailer was particularly specified for the job in order that the outfit could get under a low bridge at Stirling.

The absorption of Robsons into the United Glass Group saw a strong phase of buying Scania, a marque well liked in the previous United fleet. 'Border Scot' and 'Border Rebel' may appear to be similar 112Ms in this view, but 'Rebel' was the first six-wheeled tractive unit in the company whilst 'Scot' is a 4x2 32-tonner. The tag-axle 6x2 unit, chassis number 1082112, is used on short-haul tipper work carrying 10 loads a day of specialist silica sand used for glass making.

Still in the old livery but under new ownership, A386 NRO is chassis number 245858, being first in service during November 1983. Seen in 1984 at Tadcaster, the vehicle is being used by Robert Chicken in connection with his involvement in that famous British cycle event – The Milk Race. Chicken is a complete fanatic for both Robsons history and preserving their old Foden vehicles, currently having seven of these in his ownership. The 1937 Foden being hauled here by 'Milkmaid' was not actually an ex-Robson vehicle although it is named 'Stan Robson' as a tribute to that man. It is a DG four-wheeler and was supplied new to John Smith Ales, thus the link with the striking brewery backdrop.

good as that first 'Border Queen'. Albert Robson well remembers 'Border Supreme', collected new in 1946. Its Foden paint job should have been a sign of things to come for it was actually a distinctive red and orange, rather than the two-tone red that had been ordered. Out on the road, eight-wheeler CHH 385 was dreadfully slow. Albert says of its performance, 'It couldn't pull itself out of a wet paper bag. If you were in a hurry you had to run away and leave the thing'. He recalls dropping into Fodens every time he was passing Sandbach and asking the engineers to look under the bonnet to see if there was still an engine there. Requests to fit pedals to propel it were turned down – but thankfully fleet number FD48 was very much a one-off in the poor performance stakes.

The Robsons system of fleet numbering, which has only recently been dropped, was always rather special. The first letter was the initial from the name of the make of vehicle, e.g. F for Foden. The letter D was to denote that the engine was a diesel, P being used for petrol-engined vehicles. The numbering was straightforward, although rigid vehicles normally had two digit numbers whilst artics always had three digits.

All this numbering stood for nought with the advent of nationalization in 1949 as the Robson fleet, which then stood at about 70 in number, was close to being wiped out. Only about 14 vehicles, engaged in the milk churn collection work, weren't compulsorily purchased, so the early 1950s

was a period of stagnation in the Robson story. That time also saw Stan shipped off to a sanatorium in Switzerland for about 12 months suffering from tuberculosis; brother Thomas William Robson was to run the vehicles in his absence.

With the denationalization of some of the BRS vehicles about 1954, the Robson machine got itself back into gear. As a new trading name a third title was chosen by Stan, his first limited company name in 1936 having been Robsons (Hauliers) Ltd, replaced in 1946 by Robsons Hauliers (Carlisle) Ltd. Many other companies and titles had been formed or bought but in 1955 Robsons Border Transport Ltd was the name which was to stick for the next three decades. The 'Border' name took pride of place on the front of all the vehicles and the new colour scheme was to be the well known maroon and cream, which is only now, as the 1990s approach, being phased out in favour of a rather plain white with red lettering. Taking over the general management of the traffic was to be George Flenley, an ex-BRS man, who was to stay with Robsons until his retirement in the mid 1980s.

In 1956, as a base for his expanding operations, Stan Robson settled on a newly built depot on what was to become the Durranhill Industrial Estate. Since leaving his home at Hethersgill, the vehicles had had a variety of resting places. Working them night and day, the early motors hadn't really required garaging but at weekends they were allowed

13

'Border Hamlet' and sister vehicle 'Border Ophelia' were two Leyland Roadtrains taken by Robsons as long term demonstrators. The first two big Leylands, 'Border Galaxy' and 'Mirage' which were worked out of Carlisle, never had a brilliant reputation amongst the drivers, mainly due to lack of back-up service. But Brian Geary, fleet engineer at Flitwick, said that these two demonstrators were naturally run night and day, and the overall result of the two-year trial was reasonably impressive, back axle problems apart. C217 HOJ has chassis number JG 46199, being fitted with the L10 Cummins 290bhp engine and Fuller nine-speed gearbox. Although both 'Ophelia' and 'Hamlet' were returned to Leyland in December 1988, their use prompted an order for 16 similar tractive units from Solway Leyland DAF in Carlisle.

to park up at Hart's garage near Infirmary Road. The first main Robson base had been an old Post Office building which had also been used as a riding school in the past. The Thistle Transport purchase had also brought its garage in Durranhill road. So, one way and another, the south side of Carlisle, closely adjacent to the main truck artery, the A6 road, was always going to be the Robson home.

By 1958, the records show that Robsons had expanded dramatically to a fleet size fast approaching the three-figure mark. Although the hub of operations was always Carlisle, buying out Fred Laidlaw's premises at Haltwistle, Mill Bridge garage, provided an ideal base for the dozen or so vehicles on farm milk collection. It was also a place for the many drivers who lived out that way to park up their Carlisle-based vehicles, but their roaming pattern of work from pre-nationalization days was slowly changing.

What the nationalized carrier BRS had given to many customers throughout the country was the service of the night trunk. 'Load your goods on our vehicle even in the late afternoon and we will deliver them the next morning. Our night staff criss-cross the country on a schedule of routes which almost cover the whole mainland.' Although it wasn't a plan that Stan had invented, it was one that Robsons were to adopt and stick to. Even now, at the time of writing, almost 40% of the company's traffic runs during the night on an inter-depot network.

London and the South-east was one of the first night runs, with anything up to a dozen vehicles working south to Biggleswade for day men to take them over. A more efficient variation on that pattern saw a dozen vehicles worked north, destined for fixed changeover points which could be Stoke-on-Trent or even Doncaster, so that all drivers got back to

The only Scammell in Robsons colours, yet not one on their current Operators Licence, 'Border Bygone' is the last Scarab artic from a large fleet of similar vehicles that were used by United Glass on internal movements at their Castleford factory. Taken down to Flitwick about 1979, the vehicle was fully restored by fitting staff and is now under the care of mechanic Joe Slater who rallies it on the local Bedfordshire circuit. The Perkins P4-powered artic has a top speed of about 34mph but at this pace the vibration 'is enough to shake your eyebrows out'.

ERFs used never to figure strongly in the Robson fleet list. However with the announcement of the new 38-tonnes limit in 1983, 'Border Mammoth' and 'Border Goliath' were put into service at the heavier weight band as long-term trial vehicles. The satisfactory results prompted a further batch of C-type tractor units going into service during April/May/June 1986. 'Border Skiddaw' was the first of these nine units, having the chassis number 53200, fitted with the L10 Cummins engine and Fuller nine-speed gearbox. The ERF is pictured collecting a loaded trailer from the Durham depot. Robson's fleet once made use of part of the Elddis yard at Pity Me but has since moved to its own premises closely adjacent to the A1 at Birtley for its North-East operations.

their respective homes each night and thus couldn't claim subsistence. Once the M6 motorway was opened, Robsons worked a novel overnight shunt down to Preston. Day drivers living there would deliver into the Liverpool/Manchester areas of Lancashire then reload traffic for delivery either in Carlisle or Scotland. Back home at night, it was the job of a night man based at Carlisle to run another vehicle down to Preston and work the first one back to the depot. With such a short distance involved, the Carlisle night man was expected to do two return trips to Preston, and rigid eight-wheelers as well as artics were shuttled back and forth on this trunk.

Whilst the Robson flagships were always Fodens, the bulk of the fleet was normally more diverse, with the Ford Thames and the Thames Trader being used in large numbers. Always a vehicle that needed to be looked after, the Trader was not well suited to stand the rigours and abuse of having lots of different drivers. The D series Ford came along to replace the Traders but then, when Robsons were looking to bridge the gap between the lightweight Ford and the heavyweight Foden, the whole fleet was destined to change. After a great deal of deliberation, the company decided to try what was then the newly imported DAF 2200 range, intending to fill the middleweight gap.

When experience showed that the DAF was outperforming the Foden, Robsons had to look even more deeply at the question of fleet replacement. The revered engine of old, the Gardner, wasn't being offered by Foden in the quantities that Robsons were after, for the truck builder was promoting both the Cummins and Rolls-Royce engines in its place. It may have been a difficult decision to make but once committed the company went ahead and the maroon and cream vehicles gradually became totally Dutch dominated. 2200, 2300 and eventually 2800 tractor units were bought in great numbers, one thing in common being that all were spec'd with a day cab.

It had always been Stan Robson's belief that once his driver had done his day of work then he shouldn't spend his night in the vehicle. This opinion may have flown against convention but, as many of the vehicles were trunkers with the drivers regularly ending up at home after scheduled changeovers, it was only the few roamers who were obliged to look for overnight digs.

So the day-cab DAF became a Robson trademark nearly as distinctive as its evocative truck names. But as 1980 approached, the whole destiny of the Robson empire was in the balance. Stan Robson had never really planned it this way but as his customers like Thames Board of Workington had grown and grown, so too had the Robson fleet to keep pace with their growing demand. One of the haulier's biggest customers had been United Glass and, when Stan Robson felt the time had come to sell out as a going concern, the approach made by this favoured customer was naturally received most carefully. The wind of recession was gathering force and had Stan run the company until he died, the demand for death duties would have carved his treasured Border fleet into shreds.

The options weren't plentiful but the choice was made and in November 1980, Robsons Border Transport Ltd was acquired by the United Glass Group. You could argue that it was at this point that Robsons really became a haulier of note. For almost overnight, what had been a Carlisle-based business changed into a national concern with strategic bases throughout the country. Merging with the United Glass bases at St Helens, Castleford, Flitwick in Bedfordshire and Alloa in Scotland changed the entire potential of the company.

Massive warehousing saw massive intake and despatch of goods as Robsons left behind the small, two-ton customer and went for bulk. Even the name of the haulier was changed to Robsons Distribution Services to illustrate this entirely new concept in trading operations. A great deal of discussion had gone on prior to this decision for there were some suggestions that the name should have been United

Distribution Services. But it was agreed that 'Border Transport' should be omitted and in place of the headboard sign 'Robsons of Carlisle' the name 'Robsons' was to stand alone. What wasn't changed was the naming of the vehicles, though it was seriously considered that those based at Flitwick, Harlow and Avonmouth should be named 'Southern' rather than 'Border' to denote the national spread of operations. Fleet followers noted that this idea wasn't adopted but there was to be a small but distinctive change in the painting of the vehicles.

The newly constituted Robsons Distribution Services was split into four separate regions. Scottish was based at Alloa, Borders region at Carlisle, Northern region at St. Helens and Southern at Flitwick. Although the stamp of Robsons was to be its country-wide operation, the decal on the doors of each tractor unit incorporated the name of the vehicle's respective base for identification.

In early 1986, Stan Robson died at the age of 80. Since the moment he had sold out his business six years earlier he had ceased to have any form of contact with it. Whilst he could only be proud of its expanding influence, he was not alive to see it change hands again when the decision of United Glass was to sell it on to the Bunzl transpsort group.

Already Bunzl have had a major influence on the outward look of the Robson fleet, now numbering in excess of 200 strong. To convey a distinctive image in the competitive distribution market place, a white-based livery has been adopted in place of the traditional maroon and cream. Onlookers will note that the double-shifted day and night operation of the vehicles quickly shows in the accumulated road dirt. But whether this decision should ever be reversed is not really for an outsider to comment on.

What Stan Robson created in 1925 is about to enter the 1990s. A man who was essentially quiet and unassuming, he affected few outward trappings of his success. An exception was his Rolls-Royce motor car, changed every three years. He wanted his company to be the best in its field, like the car he drove, an ardent desire first championed by his 'Border Queen' whose successors carry onward the name of Robsons and that striving for excellence with it.

Fleet List
ROBSONS DISTRIBUTION SERVICES LTD

DAF artics

Reg no	Name	Reg no	Name	Reg no	Name	Reg no	Name
TRM 284S	Maiden	A35 SKX	Merlin	F414 FHH	Countess	CJM 753V	Sapphire
YRM 653T	Banner	B460 HAO	Bullet	F413 FHH	Phantom	JHJ 749V	Stallion
CRM 362T	Pennant	B462 HAO	Cumbrian	F412 FHH	Arrow	CJM 752V	Salute
DJH 478V	Baron	B463 HAO	Hunter	F411 FHH	Acclaim	CJM 754V	Spirit
FAO 658V	Rambler	B464 HAO	Aztec	F410 FHH	Yeoman	OMS 943W	Conquest
GAO 610V	Panther	B465 HAO	Student	F409 FHH	Minstrel	SLK 830W	Saturn
ECF 587V	Outlaw	B466 HAO	Graduate	F408 FHH	Hamlet	GGM 37W	Squire
MAO 568W	Citadel	B467 HAO	Steward	F407 FHH	Harrier	RVW 692W	Olympia
MAO 701W	Saracen	B468 HAO	Wizard	F406 FHH	Courage	PMJ 889W	Scamp
NAO 284W	Pilgrim	B469 HAO	Pegasus	F405 FHH	Prefect	WLL 147X	Mighty
OAO 320W	Emblem	B711 KAO	Deputy	F404 FHH	Nomad	A458 DAO	Mammoth
OAO 522W	Thistle	B712 KAO	Viking	F403 FHH	Sheriff	A459 DAO	Goliath
RAO 109X	Reaper	B713 KAO	Trophy	F402 FHH	Hussar	C264 PAO	Skiddaw
RHH 79X	Fiesta	B714 KAO	Rocket	F401 FHH	Pilgrim	C265 PAO	Scafell
RHH 688X	Partisan	B715 KAO	Sovereign	E512 BRM	Galaxy	C266 PAO	Langdale
YBH 398X	Scorpion	B716 KAO	Norseman	E511 BRM	Clansman	C921 PAO	Coniston
VRM 431Y	Victory	B717 KAO	Forrester	E510 BRM	Lomond	C922 PAO	Uldale
A560 EAO	Regent	B407 WBH	Scribe	E509 BRM	Cougar	C923 PAO	Caldew
A561 EAO	Century	B408 WBH	Spartan	E508 BRM	Mirage	C196 DHH	Teesdale
A562 EAO	Centurion	B409 WBH	Sultan	E507 BRM	Stuart	C197 PHH	Cheviot
A563 EAO	Citizen	B571 YGS	Ajax	E506 BRM	Sabre	C198 PHH	Kielder
A564 EAO	Knave	B572 YGS	Macbeth	E505 BRM	Colleen	F921 GAO	Elite
A565 EAO	Falcon	B573 YGS	Milkmaid	E94 BAO	Sceptre	F922 GAO	Envoy
A566 EAO	Heritage	B574 YGS	Aegis	E93 BAO	Highlander	F123 GHH	Bounty
A567 EAO	Bandit	B575 YGS	Caesar	E92 BAO	Angler	F133 GHH	Sherpa
A568 EAO	Osprey	B576 YGS	Othello	E792 XFC	Marquis	F134 GHH	Griffin
A569 EAO	Tornado	B577 YGS	Tartan			F135 GHH	Trident
A570 EAO	Melody	B578 YGS	Adonis			F136 GHH	Maestro
A572 EAO	Ranger	C201 HPP	Milkman	**ERF artics**			
A573 EAO	Amazon	C202 HPP	Avon				
A431 BHH	Champion	C203 HPP	Milkround	Reg no	Name		
A433 BHH	Prince	C281 ORM	Eden	PCP 505T	Condor		
A434 BHH	Herald	C282 ORM	Derwent	PCP 507T	Consul	**Seddon Atkinson**	
A435 BHH	Mustang	C283 ORM	Solway	OSC 563V	Award	**rigids**	
A436 BHH	Pirate	F856 DRM	Partisan	OSC 564V	Safari		
A387 NRO	Queen	F419 FHH	Tristar	XCX 398V	Viceroy	Reg no	Name
A34 SKX	Valour	F418 FHH	Migrant	XCX 435V	Laird	EYS 680T	Badger
		F417 FHH	Beaver	GNE 386V	Lord	EYS 681T	Scout

Seddon Atkinson artics

Reg no	Name
CGD 74X	Flair
CGD 75X	Charger
YCP 175Y	Comet
YCP 176Y	Cadet

Scania artics

Reg no	Name
DNF 535Y	Fox
YAO 528Y	Legion
A121 JLS	Rebel
A469 ONA	Zeus
B691 RLS	Curlew
B692 RLS	Scott
B693 RLS	Piper
B694 RLS	Grouse
B695 RLS	Mogul
B696 RLS	Hero
B697 RLS	King
B116 LEM	Sword
B117 LEM	Juno
B118 LEM	Utah
B119 LEM	Omaha
B203 UND	Gold
B204 UND	Duke
B205 UND	Renown
B206 UND	Guise
C532 NFY	Oak
C532 NFY	Redwood
C647 HRN	Beech
C648 HRN	Birch
C649 HRN	Aspen
C650 HRN	Rowan
C651 HRN	Laurel
C326 YLS	Tern

Reg no	Name
C327 YLS	Forth
C328 YLS	Clyde
C329 YLS	Tay
C330 YLS	Swan
C331 YLS	Spey
C332 YLS	Devon
C333 YLS	Esk
C334 YLS	Dee
C443 HGS	Cam
C444 HGS	City
C445 HGS	Ouse
C446 HGS	Isis
D701 DMS	Don
E765 CKX	Holly
E713 CBH	Medway
E718 CBH	Stort
E719 CBH	Thames

Volvo artics

Reg no	Name
A866 EHH	Country
A867 EHH	Tudor
A868 EHH	Hawk
A954 DAO	Javelin

Bedford pick-ups

Reg no	Name
B184 WBH	Revival
B881 RMS	Restorer

Bedford Astramax

Reg no	Name
C259 AMS	Remedy
C478 FNM	Response
C623 DAO	Valet

Ford rigid

Reg no	Name
MGA 95A	Shuttle

Ford Transit

Reg no	Name
SHH 458X	Rescue
B529 VHY	Courier

Leyland Sherpa

Reg no	Name
RFC 944T	Hornet

Leyland

Reg no	Name
F973 FRM	Trent
F975 FRM	Dandy
F976 FRM	Saxon
F977 FRM	Romany
F978 FRM	Dragoon
F979 FRM	Glory
F980 FRM	Artisan
F981 FRM	Sniper
F982 FRM	Chariot
F983 FRM	Cairn
F817 GAO	Hermes
F819 GAO	Claudius
F820 GAO	Titan
F822 GAO	Patriot

2: Moreton C. Cullimore & Son Ltd

In the field of naming trucks perhaps the strangest identities are those affixed to the two-tone green vehicles of Cullimores of Stroud. Written on the doors in a flowing script fashion, the name often has to be carefully pondered over simply to decipher it. Once you realize you are looking at 'Jefferson Brick', 'Mr Justice Starleigh' or even 'Dr Alexandre Manette', you begin to want to know something about the history of Cullimores so that you can understand why the names from the books of Charles Dickens are affixed to these Gloucestershire-based lorries.

Like Stan Robson before him, Moreton C. Cullimore started out in road haulage using the modest means of a converted Model T Ford. Frampton-born Cullimore must have been a pioneer in his day for it was recorded that, running his vehicle out of Ferris Court, Lypiatt, he was only the second person in Gloucestershire to have transported livestock by mechanical means.

The fleet was to increase when Moreton met up with Tom Morris and began hauling gravel on his behalf out of the pits around Frampton. The relationship was strengthened when Cullimores acted as merchants on Morris's behalf for customers in the Stroud area. In 1936, Cullimore bought his own land at South Cerney and began winning gravel on his own account.

Opposite: right up until the middle 1940s, Cullimores relied on four-wheeled tippers to haul their cargo. With a view to expanding their carrying potential, Moreton Cullimore bought HDG 554 in 1946. Rather over spec'd for sand and gravel haulage, the long-nosed Thornycroft had originally been intended as a mobile crane chassis. Although it had underbody tipping gear, Cullimores had it fitted with a wooden double-dropside body so that general cargo could be carried if needed. The vehicle was supplied by Wilson Scott of Gloucester who were later to be taken over by the Lex Group. Above: when Cadburys set up premises in nearby Frampton, Cullimores invested in suitable vehicles to carry their chocolate brickettes. The carefully sheeted loads of partially refined cocoa were hauled to Bournville in Birmingham for further refinement into Cadbury's well known products. This 1960 Commer with its distinctive opposed-piston two-stroke engine was also Cullimores' first outfit to have a Taskers of Andover semi-trailer fitted with an automatic coupling. Below: this Foden line-up seen in 1961 illustrates Cullimores' first Foden on the far left and their latest Sandbach purchase parked next to it. The line up of drivers from left to right are Graham Shipway, Frank Winfield, Harold Trinder, Ray Winston and Jimmy Watkins. JDD 301 was put on the road in 1948 and 13 years later it had half a million hard miles to its credit with Frank Winfield normally behind the helm. Cullimores tended to hang onto their driving staff. Jimmy Watkins started as a relief driver when he agreed to do a fortnight's work in 1946 – and finished this period of relief work in 1985 when he retired. Apart from the front-step-entry four-wheeler on the right, the vehicles were all eight-wheelers excepting UDG 309, which was a 'Chinese Six' platform.

Rather than being traded-in or sold once it has come to the end of its roadgoing career, a tipper is expected to work even harder on the private roads of Cullimores' gravel pits. This 1964 Guy Warrior is seen in 1974 at the Ashton Keynes quarry, having managed to survive its ten hard years of work in reasonable condition, sun visor apart. Cullimores took delivery of the Guy, chassis number 4427, on October 22, 1964. It is interesting to note the basic price of £2,759, inflated to a final invoice bill of £3,239; amongst the extra charges was £75 for the fitment of automatic chassis lubrication, £12 10s for flashing indicators and a £10 delivery charge.

The general haulage side of the business expanded up to maximum weight artics, and normally Foden tractive units were utilized. However the lengthy waiting time following an order for a Foden meant that Cullimores sometimes had to turn elsewhere when they wanted a vehicle in a hurry. The company never ran many AECs though – in fact 'Fagin' was their only one. It wasn't kept too long, and it is recalled that Moreton Cullimore was rather disgusted with it for its engine only lasted 100,000 miles. Timber still forms a big part of Cullimores' platform-borne traffic both into and out of its main Warminster depot.

By 1939, rapid expansion of the fleet had seen it grow well into double figures, mainly four-wheeled Bedford and Canadian Dodge tippers. During the war, construction work took on a more serious nature and, like many others, Cullimore had half his fleet seconded down into Devon and Cornwall on airfield building. The separation of the two halves of his fleet meant Cullimore spent a great deal of his time on the move, travelling between them, one reason why at that time he was nicknamed 'Caravan Cullimore'.

Following the pattern of the wartime years, when road signs, place names and the like were removed or painted out to confuse any invading enemy, all the tipper lorries being used on construction work were painted in the same identical drab green finish. With 400-plus vehicles involved, it thus became extremely difficult for Cullimore, like every other owner, to identify his own vehicles from everyone else's when he came down to service, repair or even just meet up with the seconded driving staff.

Moreton had noticed that some of the aircraft in use by the RAF had been personalized with painted names, so he hit on the idea of naming his own vehicles. To ensure it didn't upset the authorities, the names were painted very small either on top of the radiator or on the vehicle's headboard. As a source of names, Cullimore resorted to the books of Charles Dickens, a man, he felt, who always let right prevail.

Although Cullimores have had a great number of long-serving drivers, the retirement of Frank Winfield in the summer of 1973 was still a big occasion which prompted celebrating in the prescribed manner. Frank is pictured towards the centre of this staff line-up and perhaps it reflects the era he comes from that he is the only one wearing a cap. He drove the first diesel-engined vehicle to come new to Cullimores and was only to drive two other Foden tippers in all his service. He is quoted as saying in 1961 when he got his last Foden, 'Well Guv'nor, this'll just about see me out to retirement' and it did in fact do just that.

At the end of the war, the need for these individual identities was gone and the practice faded out as Cullimores became more and more involved in construction projects throughout the area. Most notable of these was the supply of 300,000 tons of material used in the construction of the runway at Filton for the giant prototype Brabazon airliner. The buying of more land meant future sand and gravel winning was assured, and the Cullimore fleet took on two distinct patterns as continued diversification in the general haulage side of the business always meant there was to be a 50-50 split between that and their own account traffic.

In 1961, Moreton's son Roger came into the business and with him he brought a high degree of training in the building and structural engineering trade which he soon put to use in developing the company's abilities. Roger also decided to revive the wartime tradition of naming the vehicles, still in the Dickens mould. With Fodens favoured as the fleet heavyweights since the early 1950s, suitably dignified names were selected for the eight-wheelers like 'Captain Edward Cuttle', 'General Choke' or the heroic 'Sydney Carton'.

Augmenting the aggregates business, Cullimores went into the production and delivery of concrete, with plants at Ashton Keynes and Netherhills. Naturally a favoured name regularly kept in use for one of the mobile truck mixers is 'Oliver Twist'. The naming process has been extended to what would otherwise appear as rather mundane items of plant and it gives a machine like an International loading shovel far more presence to be called 'Sir Joseph Bowley'.

Even the company's Smiths dragline excavator is called 'Thomas Traddles'. The pick of the bunch, however, must be the Aveling Barford road roller adorned with the title 'Sir Leicester Dedlock'.

Throughout the 1960s father and son worked closely together to develop the company which was to include amongst its interests a tyre distribution business in Bristol. During the summer of 1969 Roger took overall control of Cullimores, although Moreton continued to give guidance until his death in May 1972.

Although the administrative centre of Cullimores is still at 47, London Road, Stroud, the physical transport side of the business now revolves round the ideally placed developing site at Netherhills. Originally very close to the A38 trunk road, and now with junction 13 of the M5 motorway only about a mile away, the brand new purpose-built workshop is already providing contract maintenance to distant-based haulier's vehicles. As well as embracing a concrete batching plant, workshops and ample storage facilities, the Netherhills depot is also a base for Cotswold Enterprises. This independent company makes wooden pallets and employs 15 people, delivery of their finished product being via Cullimore vehicles.

The Cullimore fleet of the late 1980s has changed a great deal from that of 20 years earlier. A fleet once led by Foden multi-wheelers now has just a sole representative from Foden, and that used as a recovery vehicle. The remainder of the '60s fleet was mostly four-wheelers of Albion, Dodge,

21

By the summer of 1969 Roger Cullimore had taken over the running of the company from Moreton. Both father and son are pictured outside the Foden works at Sandbach with Arthur Hassle, the sales manager responsible for the Gloucestershire area. They are taking delivery of an eight-wheeled tipper chassis on the left and a 4x2 general haulage tractive unit on the right. The tractor was to receive the name 'Colonel Diver'. The smaller headboard of the newer cab design has meant that the company name has had to be shortened, but Foden have also mistakenly rendered it as '& Sons', the tipper cab showing the correct singular form.

With an increase in the demand for aggregates at the start of the 1970s to supply the motorway building boom, Cullimores commissioned a new washing plant at Ashton Keynes. Charlie Hall is pictured with his new Gardner-powered eight-wheeled Foden tipper, 'Tim Linkenwater', taking the first load from the plant. Charlie joined the company in 1939 and was to retire in 1985. His vehicle is fitted with a Neville U-shaped body which has been insulated to allow for the carriage of Tarmac when the sand and gravel work was quite.

Leyland Bison 'Wackford Squeers' is seen when new about 1981 to illustrate the latest type of Neville-Charrold tipper body that was being fitted to the fleet vehicles. Roger Cullimore had first met George Neville at the Commercial Motor Show in 1960. Although for lighter applications Cullimores used wooden bodies, when it came to a hard and demanding work pattern, Neville bodies were always specified even when the original company had a change of ownership. Cullimores, like many others, were never really happy with the fixed-head Leyland engine at this period and later examples of the Constructor 6, the subsequent Bison replacement, were to be specified with a DAF 825 engine.

Commer and Leyland makes. Leyland is still strongly represented, but the four-wheeler type has been almost completely ousted in preference for more potential payload from a smaller number of six and eight-wheeled tippers. Whilst the rigids are a healthy mixture of Leyland, Volvo and DAF, the artic line up – nominal Volvo presence apart – has long been based on ERF four-wheeled maximum-weight tractor units.

When Fodens passed into the ownership of the Paccar concern, Roger didn't take to the new parent's offerings so decided to go to the other truck builder in Sandbach. The Volvo units were bought mainly to show ERF that Cullimores could of course buy other makes if they so desired and keep the element of competition in this sector of the fleet alive. Cullimores have long specified Rolls-Royce engines for the ERF tractors, the latest having the Perkins-badged ones. Whilst these artics are part of a normal replacement cycle, Cullimores tend to get an entire life out of their tippers. Once they are no longer suitable for longer distance roadwork, they are expected to work even harder,

albeit over shorter distances, on internal work in one of the Cullimore quarries. With a view to getting extended life from the favoured Leyland multi-wheelers, Cullimores have taken delivery of the latest Constructor 6 machines fitted with the DAF power pack.

Cullimores are always ready to try something different if they feel it will improve efficiency and so take every chance to utilize demonstration vehicles offered to them. They often go on to buy the demonstrators; 'Barnaby Rudge', their sole ERF eight-wheeled rigid tipper came in this fashion, as did 'Ernest Defarge', the first Volvo F10 artic tractor unit.

The fleet is a rare mixture of old and new stretching from the newest variant from Leyland-DAF to the oldest version of Scammell Pioneer, 'Dr. Alexandre Manette', used as a recovery vehicle. 'Major Bagshot' is a recently finished restoration project, an S21 Foden four-wheeled tipper which has been stamped at the Cartmarking Ceremony held annually at the Guildhall in the City of London. That is quite an award for a member of this named classic fleet.

Fleet List
MORETON C. CULLIMORE & SON LTD

General haulage fleet

Reg no	Make/type	Dickens name
F280 RDG	ERF	Captain Edward Cuttle
F279 RDG	ERF	General Cyrus Choke
E904 MAD	ERF	Serjeant Snubbin
E158 KAD	ERF	Bob Crachit
C770 WDD	ERF	Captain Boldwig
C769 WDD	ERF	Mr Tulkingham
A935 FDD	Volvo	Prince Leopold
YDG 502Y	Volvo	Ernest Defarge
FTU 221X	ERF	Major Tpschoffski
TDG 770X	ERF	Harry Charker
GDG 541V	ERF	Captain James Harthouse
CDD 98T	ERF	James Steerforth
VDG 118S	ERF	Colonel Groper
WDF 751S	ERF	Josiah Bounderby
NDD 340P	ERF	Abel Magwitch
JAD 633N	Foden	Sir Barnett Skettles

Artic tippers

Reg no	Make/type	Dickens name
PDW 6Y	ERF	Sir Charles Rampart
XFH 36S	ERF	Sir John Fielding

Eight-wheelers

Reg no	Make/type	Dickens name
(new)	ERF	Mr Bumble
F714 RDG	Constructor	Tim Linkinwater
E757 GFH	Constructor	Lord Frederick Verisopht
F206 OFH	Constructor	Sir Dingleby Dabber
D453 FDF	DAF	Sir Thomas Clubber
C180 YDD	DAF	Captain Purday
B995 RDF	DAF	Mr Justice Stareleigh
A574 KDF	DAF	Martin Chuzzlewit
A922 FDD	Volvo	Lord George Gordon
YDG 512Y	Volvo	Baron Von Swillenhausen
MGM 276X	DAF	Jeremiah Flintwinch
NAD 976W	Leyland	Dick Datchery
KDD 392V	Leyland	Daniel Dancer
JAD 758V	ERF	Barnaby Rudge

Six-wheelers

Reg no	Make/type	Dickens name
(new)	Volvo	David Copperfield
D799 EDF	Constructor	Sir Thomas Blazo
D124 AFH	Constructor	Fagin
A933 FDD	Volvo	Doctor Strong
YDG 417Y	Constructor	Jacob Marley
WDD 797X	Bison	John Westlock
OFH 98W	Bison	Wackford Squeers
FDF 747T	Bison	Mr Mantalini
AFH 459T	Reiver	Daniel Peggotty

Four-wheelers

Reg no	Make/type	Dickens name
OFH 97W	Clydesdale	Sydney Carton

Concrete fleet

Reg no	Make/type	Dickens name
E905 MAD	Constructor	Nathaniel Pipkin
D125 AFH	Constructor	Slasher
B123 NDF	Constructor	Oliver Twist
WFH 263X	Bison	Mr Dombey
CDD 653T	Bison	Captain Jack Bunsby
GWS 925N	Bison	Mr Dick

Light vehicles

Reg no	Make/type	Dickens name
A412 KAD	Peugeot p/u	Noddy Boffin
A369 KDD	Peugeot p/u	Noah Claypole
CAD 846Y	Sherpa van	Serjeant Buzfuz
VAD 166X	Bedford p/u	Mr Pickwick
NAD 980W	Sherpa p/u	Sara Gamp
ODD 935W	Sherpa	Charles Cheeryble
AAE 793V	Datsun p/u	Bill Sikes
EDF 631T	Sherpa van	Toots

Vintage

Reg no	Make/type	Dickens name
6074 DD	Foden	Major Bagstock
unreg'd.	Scammell Pioneer	Dr Alexandre Manette

Breakdown vehicle

Reg no	Make/type	Dickens name
Q381 FDD	Foden	Sir Mulberry Hawk

Plant machines and work trucks

Reg no	Make/type	Dickens name
C422 VDF	520 loading shovel	Sir Joseph Bowley
C421 VDF	MAN dump truck	Nicodemus Dumps
B45 PAD	Bray loading shovel	Benjamin Britain
A156 HDD	Schaeff loader	Mr Rokesmith
Unreg'd.	530 loading shovel	William Swidger
XDG 624X	Foden dump truck	Trotty Veck
XDG 625X	MAN dump truck	Little Nell
VAD 513X	Kamatsu dozer shovel	Little Dorrit
Unreg'd.	Hydraulic excavator	The Artful Dodger
Unreg'd.	Dragline excavator	Inspector Bucket
BAD 168T	M/Ferguson loader	Mr Fezziwig
BAD 169T	M/Ferguson loader	Mr Anthony Humm
Unreg'd.	Yumbo 635 excavator	Coppernose
YHR 855T	Lansing Bagnall forklift truck	Tom Pinch
ODG 328	Merton loading shovel	Job Trotter
TDD 275R	Leyland Bison tipper	Captain Blunderbore
RDD 850M	Foden pit lorry	Jaggers
Unreg'd.	38 RB excavator	John Browdie
WAD 692J	Aveling Barford road roller	Sir Leicester Dedlock
Unreg'd.	Excavator	Thomas Traddles
GDF 503N	Foden pit lorry	Major Hannibal Chollop
Unreg'd.	530 loading shovel	Harold Skimpole
AAD 333S	Winget dumper	(not named)

3: Pollock (Scotrans) Ltd

Close to losing its own identity and becoming just a suburb of Edinburgh, the town of Musselburgh has since 1954 been the base of operations for the resplendent fleet of Pollocks. It is the colour scheme of torquoise, blue and red which makes this mix of Scania, Mercedes and DAF outfits, currently just on 30 in number, such a distinctive sight wherever they go. Pollock's beat nowadays is mainly between Edinburgh and the south coast of England but it was simply local cartage that started the company founder William G.D. Pollock as an owner driver in 1935. He worked out of Corstorphine – on the other side of Edinburgh – at that time and prospered by giving good and loyal service, so the fleet grew to 16 in number by 1949 and the advent of nationalization.

It was a thoroughbred fleet with ERF predominating but also featuring both Leyland and Vulcan vehicles. All were to be taken under the British Road Services banner. The attributes of William Pollock himself were soon identified and he rose to be Group Manager of the East Lothian & Borders Group of BRS, based at Haddington with 13 local depots under his control.

Controlling 224 vehicles kept Pollock busy but the enjoyment of running his own business was an even bigger attraction. In 1954, with the relaxation of partial denationalization, Pollock left his managerial job, buying some vehicles and licences from the BRS empire. The name of William G.D. Pollock was proudly emblazoned in true Scottish style down the cabs of his vehicles and by 1960 the fleet had grown to 23 platforms. The growth in size merited the need to establish the trading company of Pollock (Musselburgh) Ltd, the registered office being at 101, Newbigging.

The constraints of operator licensing prior to 1968 meant that expansion could be a very slow process but in 1963 the Pollock fleet almost doubled with the acquisition of 23 vehicles from Dalkeith Transport & Storage Co Ltd. It was not a total sell-out by this adjacent haulier, as Dalkeith remained in transport but purely on the livestock and agricultural side.

The Pollocks fleet of the 1960s featured some of the classic vehicles of the period. Whilst Albion Reiver and AEC Marshall six-wheelers may have been liked for their lightness and appetite for work, it was to be the Gardner-powered Atkinson eight-wheelers that championed the name of Pollocks up and down the Great North Road. Artics were introduced into the fleet in the early 1960s and especially after 1965 with the advent of 32-tonners, for their potential payload was certainly higher than the equivalent rigids. But what kept the four and six-wheelers running on long distance work was the fact that some of the long established customers' premises both in London and Edinburgh were simply not large enough to accept anything more than the smaller rigids.

From the mid-1950s, the London trunk was the backbone of the Pollock traffic and even then, with such a small fleet, two vehicles a night were making that regular 8pm departure. Paper and rope were their staple outward-bound cargo. To ensure they got enough back loads, Pollocks were involved in setting up their own London-based company.

At its outset Express Carriers Ltd was formed with equal interests to Pollocks, Munroes of Aberdeen, Russells of Bathgate and Dalkeith Transport & Storage. But with the changing fortunes of Russells and Dalkeith, these two hauliers left the arrangement. With Munroes preferring the Aberdeen and Highland back loads, that left the lowlands and Border traffic to Pollocks. Primarily intended to capture traffic to service the Scottish-based fleets, Express Carriers have in fact always run a couple of vehicles in their own livery as well.

With the Pollock fleet growing, the family influence also strengthened as William's two sons George and Ian became

The central core of the road transport nationalization policy was the requisition of well established long-distance fleets like Pollocks who worked out of Corstorphine in the late 1940s. Founder of the company William Pollock, is seen here standing in front of his premium fleet which was predominately ERFs, although both Vulcan and Leyland vehicles were also used. The photograph dates from about 1950 and although no time has been allowed yet for a total fleet repaint, items like the added fleet number prefix ELG – East Lothian Group – plus a British Road Services headboard on the third ERF in line, clearly indicate that ownership of the vehicles had passed to the government Road Haulage Executive.

The Atkinson eight-wheeler was the flagship of the Pollock fleet at the start of the 1960s, 9797 SF being the last in a quartet which included similar eight-leggers 33 SC, 88 SC and 3722 SC. This Frank Richardson photograph taken on August 8, 1968 finds 'Night Scotsman' parked up overnight, back-loading with bricks from Tyneside. The Atkinson, first on the road in 1963, displays the Colquhoun tartan.

actively involved in the business. It is Ian Pollock who takes credit for starting to name the Pollock vehicles in a very individual manner about 1963. Whilst the basic livery of Pollocks was taken as inspiration by many other operators – including the showmen of Crows – the distinctive Pollock trademark was to be an individual name painted on top of a true Scottish tartan. The first names were applied to some AEC Mammoth Majors which had the whole of the grille painted in tartan. This concept didn't lend itself to the shape of every vehicle in the fleet so the idea of placing a scroll of tartan at the top or around the grille was adopted. The individual name of the vehicle was then sign-written on top of the tartan band.

Ian first took his inspiration for names from famous railway engines or trains like 'Flying Scot' but with close to 60 vehicles to adorn he added a strange mix of evocative Scottish names, TV programmes and even titles of contemporary pop songs. Examples were 'Scotia's Pride' on JSG 606E, an AEC Marshall six-wheeled rigid, 'Cannonball' on ASC 780B, an Atkinson Silver Knight artic, and 'Day Tripper', the famous Beatles song title, affixed to FSF 140D, an AEC Mercury artic.

The expansion of the 1960s saw a major broadening in the horizons of Pollocks traffic. Whilst six tankers were to be used around the Edinburgh area for the delivery of fuel oil, the long distance men were finding more traffic sourced out of Glasgow and Coatbridge being destined for Birmingham and the Midlands. To manage this change in traffic flow

Frank Richardson recorded Geordy and Ian sheeting this load of paper at the Musselburgh depot on Saturday, September 7, 1968. 'Cannonball' dates from March 1964, and was named after an American series shown on television in the early 1960s that featured strongly a Detroit-powered GMC artic. Also seen in shot is one of the two 3-ton Bedfords, named 'Trailtrekker' and 'Pathfinder', used by Pollock drivers too young to drive HGVs. What appears to be the top of a bus in the background is 'Moby Dick', a crew-cabbed AEC Matador 4x4 recovery vehicle.

Acquired specifically to haul coiled steel from Gartcosh in Glasgow on an overnight trunk down to the Midlands, this trio of ERF tractors, all named after television programmes, shows the slight variation in cabs fitted in 1964. The tractor units on the outside, with Cummins engines, have the door-over-wheel cab entry, whilst the centre ERF has the Gardner 6LX 150 engine and front-step cab. AWS 412B 'Thunderbird' was eventually to be sold on by Pollocks to Direct Transport of Shildon.

One vehicle of the Pollock fleet that was never to receive a name was this Morris van used for local fetching and carrying around the Edinburgh area. The distinctive logo was also featured on this vehicle's subsequent replacement, a Commer Walk Thru van, NSF 700G. The fleet number of 54 is indicative of the size of the Pollock fleet about 1965. It was to peak at about the 64 mark, having expanded greatly after the acquisition of the haulage interests of Dalkeith Transport & Storage Co.

Although Pollocks were to haul whisky in bulk in the late 1970s, ten years earlier than that they carried a very different liquid, running a number of maximum-weight artic tankers on local black oil distribution. Four were on contract to Shell, five on contract to Shaws Fuels and one for Stephenson Clarke. The stainless steel tank pictured was lagged to keep up the interior temperature. The tractor seen here, 'Early Bird', is recalled by Pollock followers as more normally coupled to a platform semi-trailer. ESF 404C, named after a space satellite, had the McLaren tartan and was also fitted with four fairy lights on top of the headboard, a company trade-mark long before the idea became the vogue.

new depots were opened at both Coatbridge and Birmingham.

By 1971, the Pollock fleet had grown to 65 strong, along with 75 semi-trailers, and William Pollock sensed it was time to consider the future of his company. In the event of his sudden demise, the claim for estate duty would have been particularly costly, so the reluctant decision was made to sell the company as a going concern and in July 1971, Pollock (Musselburgh) Ltd was acquired by Ralph Hilton Transport Services Ltd in a share deal worth £260,400.

The Hilton group had acquired a considerable reputation for their dramatic expansion in the late 1960s and, with the Pollock purchase, embraced a total of 60 different companies running 1,800 vehicles. Pollocks continued to have a strong influence in the Hilton group (later to be named Roadships Ltd), being one of the few profitable companies in that empire. The fleet retained its own livery and identity whilst father and two sons remained on the board and ran the business just as though it was their own.

The links that the Pollock family had formed with their operations were not to be broken easily and when, in July 1975, the Roadships group went into receivership, they took swift and immediate steps to buy back the massive chunk of Pollock (Musselburgh) Ltd assets from the receiver. For complicated business reasons the old name of the company couldn't be retained but as Pollock (Scotrans) Ltd the

This AEC photograph shows 'Day Tripper' passing through Fort William part-loaded with paper from Kent. Named after the famous Beatles pop song of the era, the tractor unit dates from March 1966 and was one of five similar Ergomatic-cabbed Mercurys run at that time, out of a fleet total of 13 AECs. Featuring the Macleod of Lewis tartan, the outfit is passing the Gaelic sign indicating Mary Macintyre's shop.

Frank Richardson found 'Lively Lady' outside the Musselburgh depot on Sunday, October 13, 1968, prior to heading south with its load of paper from a mill in Edinburgh that Pollocks still haul for, 20 years on. Even though the company was running maximum-weight eight-wheeled rigids and artics at that time, they still trunked and tramped all over the country with the smaller six-wheelers. Regular driver of this well chromed Marshal was George Wright who had only taken delivery of it six weeks prior to the date of the photograph. Named after a record-breaking boat, the AEC has the Chisholm tartan painted on it.

Above: Express Carriers of London was formed originally as a clearing-house concern, mainly to provide Scotland-bound traffic for its four joint owners; Russells of Bathgate, Dalkeith Transport, Munros of Aberdeen and Pollocks. The first two hauliers were to leave the association leaving the latter two to share the traffic, normally on a Highlands/Lowlands basis when at all possible. The company did run one or two vehicles in its own colours, their first Atkinson being named 'Apollo 7' after the American space satellite. Brothers George (on the left) and Ian Pollock are standing beside these Express DAF 2800 tractor units which are coupled to Pollocks own Crown Lock Vans: as the name suggests the semi-trailers were normally used for the bonded carriage of whisky. Below: the recent Pollock fleet includes a solid sector of DAF vehicles, and although they are mainly articulated, two rigid DAF FAS 2105 DHR six-wheelers have also been run. The main reasoning behind this was that long-serving drivers like George Wright never qualified for the Class 1 type of HGV driving licence and to ensure they had a vehicle to drive legally on their Class 2 licences, Pollocks continued to purchase these smaller rigid vehicles. Ian Pollock is seen in Leith Docks behind the wheel of 'Olympic' which was a sister vehicle to a similar six-wheeled DAF, 'Greased Lightning'.

During 1979-1980, Pollocks were to take delivery of six TR305 Berliet/Renault 4x2 tractor units. Geoff Milne, recognized as an authority on named trucks, was asked to suggest a suitable name for the company's first French vehicle and as the thistle had always been a strong part of the Pollock livery, he choose the title 'Fleur D'Ecosse', French for Flower of Scotland. Pollock followers will spot that the registration OSG 666V is merely a mock fitted for the Renault photograph, and in fact this tractor was to be registered PFS 645V on September 1, 1979. The paintwork featured the Stewart dress form of tartan. The semi-trailer it pulls here is loaded with empty whisky barrels heading north for replenishment.

Pollock name and vehicles continued to work for established customers with only one weekend lost while the vehicles were in the hands of the receiver.

It was business almost as usual, but the general make-up of the fleet in the 1970s had changed dramatically from that of the 1960s. Whilst ERFs continued to linger on, the Atkinsons and AECs were replaced with imports as Scania 110s became the standard Pollock workhorses. Ford vehicles also appeared in Pollocks colours after November 1976 when the company acquired the assets of R.S. Pirnie of Pitlochry. Pirnies had specialized in the movement of bulk whisky so Pollocks continued this type of traffic with articulated tankers like 'Globetrotter', a Transcontinental

registered JSR 102P.

Ian Pollock was now taking an even bigger role in the running of the company, and he regularly turned to Geoff Milne to provide inspiration for some new names. Geoff, from Chester-le-Street, had been an enthusiastic follower of the Pollock fleet since 1963 and was recognized as an authority on named fleets. His affinity to Pollocks was reflected in the name 'Jingling Geordie' that was coined by the company to mark this Tynesider's marriage in 1979 and applied to one of their Scanias.

In 1981 Pollocks moved across the town to their current premises in Olivebank. The fleet of the '80s has now consolidated at the 30 mark, most being maximum-weight

When first running at the newly introduced 38-tonnes weight band, Pollocks opted for the 2+3 axle configuration. Further rethinking of this strategy saw them change towards the six-wheeled tractor unit, 'Untouchable' being their first Mercedes 6x2. The name of the tractor was inherited from the company's first six-wheeled tractor unit, an Atkinson RAS registered KWS 666F, and came from a well known television programme of the mid-1960s. Regular driver of this Mercedes is Peter Wight who lives 60 miles south of the company's HQ, in Kelso. The 2035S Powerliner has EPS gearchanging and is normally coupled to a curtainsider semi-trailer.

artics. Scania are still highly favoured although DAF, Renault, Mercedes and ERF are utilized too. With the announcement of the 38-tonnes limit in 1983, Pollocks first favoured the 2+3 combination in the guise of 'Rolling Thunder', a DAF 3300 registered A770 YSG. The company had been running the 40-tonne type of tractor unit prior to the change in weights so that seemed the easiest option to follow. However with anything up to 17 drops on their back when they leave the Musselburgh base destined for the south of England, the prospect of drive-axle overloads as the vehicle was gradually unloaded became a frightening reality. To counteract that threat, Pollocks now run most of their 38-tonners in the 3+2 mode.

The isolated exceptions to the fully articulated fleet are some rigid six-wheelers which stay on the strength because their respective drivers do not have Class One HGV driving licences. In the lead-up time to the new HGV licensing system in the later 1960s, these men normally drove rigid eight-wheelers so under the 'grandfather's rights' system they only qualified for a Class Two licence. Some of them were rather set in their ways and didn't really want to take the Class One test so the company decided to keep buying the odd rigid so that they would have a vehicle to drive. As and when these drivers come up for retirement, the rigids will probably be phased out of the fleet.

This loyalty to their staff is reflected in the number of sons who have followed their respective fathers into the Pollock driving line-up. The tradition of the family is very much a Pollock hallmark; at 80 years old William Pollock still took an active interest in the company before he died. With George leaving to run his own hotel business, the fleet is now under the control of Ian Pollock. Ian's son Scott has now joined the company, the prospect being that the family tradition is destined to continue ever onward.

Fleet List
POLLOCK (Scotrans) LTD

Fleet no	Reg no	Make & model		Axles	GVW*	Registered	Name
1	B202 KSF	Mercedes	1633	2	38	1/01/86	Grand Slam
2	E21 JSF	Scania	112	3	38	10/09/87	Oor Wullie
3	B806 KSX	Scania	112	2	38	1/02/85	Nordic Invader
4	E151 HSC	Mercedes	307D	2 (p/u)	3.5	1/08/87	-
5	B30 LSF	DAF	3300	2	38	1/03/85	Discovery
6	C515 PSG	Mercedes	1633	2	38	1/08/85	Scotia's Pride
7	C221 USG	Renault	T310	2	38	1/02/86	Atlantis
8	C800 USX	Renault	T310	2	38	1/03/86	French Connection
9	C808 USX	Renault	T310	2	38	1/04/86	Bergerac
10	A313 BSC	DAF	3300	2	38	1/11/83	Thrust II
11	A350 ASF	Mercedes	1628	2	38	4/10/83	Challenger
12	A414 YFS	Mercedes	1628	2	38	2/09/83	Iolair
14	E94 JSG	Mercedes	2035	3	38	11/09/87	Untouchable
15	C259 MPU	Scania	P92	3	24	20/06/86	-
16	SSF 665Y	Mercedes	1628	2	32	1/02/83	Globetrotter
17	RSG 707Y	Mercedes	1628	2	32	12/11/82	Hermes
18	E22 JSF	Scania	112	3	38	1/11/87	Highland Express
19	F363 TSC	Mercedes	2035	3	38	19/08/88	Two Capitals
20	F434 RSG	Mercedes	-	-	3.5	1/10/88	-
21	PSG 480Y	DAF	3300	2	32	1/09/82	Invincible
22	A888 BSX	Mercedes	1628	2	38	1/01/84	Knight Rider
23	OSF 633Y	Mercedes	1628	2	32	1/08/82	Four Seasons
24	B900 GSG	Mercedes	1628	2	38	1/08/84	Royal Highland
25	A770 YSG	DAF	3300	2	38	2/09/82	Rolling Thunder
26	F821 USX	ERF	E6	2	17	1/11/88	Jingling Geordie
27	PSC 560Y	DAF	3300	2	32	13/08/82	Chariots of Fire
28	A139 XSX	Leyland Terrier		2	7.5	1/01/84	-
29	B347 MFS	Leyland Freighter		2	16	1/03/85	-
30	MSG 757X	DAF	3300	2	32	7/06/82	Flying Dutchman
31	TSG 701V	Scania	111	2	32	1/03/80	Dallas
32**	USA 697S	Atkinson RR220		2	32	9/09/77	Braw Scott

* Tonnes   ** Show vehicle only.

4: Sutton & Son (St. Helens) Ltd

Of all the things that can influence the formation and the running of a road transport concern, time and time again the most important and the most enduring turns out to be the family connection. Father may have started up the business but so often it is son and then even grandson who takes it on and develops the original idea and takes advantage of the opportunities presented by changing circumstances. The family tradition remains the cornerstone. This is the pattern to be seen in the story of one of the country's most famous distribution operations, Suttons of St Helens, though in their case it was the formidable figure of mother who first got them into the transport business.

Alice Beatrice Sutton, large in stature and very strong willed, is recalled as a marvellous woman by those who knew her. Number 7, Lea Green Road, St Helens was home for her, three sons and a daughter – but making 4 gallons of tea a day as well as countless bacon sandwiches meant it was open house to all in the neighbourhood. Having the only telephone in the area, Alice was for ever running one message or shouting another into that corded wonder that hung on the wall. As a business, she bought coal in bulk from the local colliery and then sold it on in smaller sacked deliveries. Having one horse and cart meant a limited amount of work which was curtailed even further during the warm summer months and by 1923 she was close to packing the business in altogether, had it not been for the intervention of her youngest son Alfred.

Just sacked from the local pit after hitting the foreman who had called him a bastard, the young 16-year-old had a fair bit of natural business sense as well as a very strong streak of dignity and pride. Negotiating a year's credit with all his suppliers – the pit, the farrier and the farmer who supplied the horse's feed – he turned the business round and began carrying stone into Liverpool with an expanding fleet.

By 1929 Alf had met up with one Soly Royal who owned Ex-Army Transport Ltd amongst his diverse interests. Alf was fascinated by what the new generation of lorries could haul when compared to his single-horse-power cart and took little persuasion to sign his life away on the HP by investing in DJ 5152, an exceptionally strong Leyland Hippo six-wheeler. Running a clearing house, Soly also guaranteed Alf traffic, less his nominal percentage, of course, until Alf realised that Soly was taking him to the cleaners. 'I'm only donating a ha'penny a ton to charity,' was Soly's begging cry – but the threatening confrontation certainly meant Suttons' rates were improved. In 1935, Alf bought a Leyland Cub, BC 3099, for £165, and two years later he was to buy his first brand new vehicle, a gleaming AEC Mammoth Major eight-wheeler.

Alf took Fred Craig up to Burnley on the back of his motorbike to collect the new AEC from dealers Oswald Tillotson. Stowing the motorbike up against the lorry's headboard for the return journey, Fred asked if he could drive. The eight-legger at that time was quite an innovation and people regularly asked, 'Do all the wheels go round?' such was the fascination at seeing so many tyres. Alf was keen himself to have a go but reluctantly took to the passenger seat as Fred jumped up behind the wheel. Not really used to an AEC, Fred grated the gears a time or two as he manoeuvred the big rigid round, which brought stares of anguish from the Tillotson man. Going for reverse, he grated the gear cogs again which prompted the white-coat man into action. 'What's your name?' he asked Fred as he pulled out his pencil and pad, 'I'm going to report you to Mr Sutton, I'm sure he won't want to employ a driver like you,' a remark which brought a broad grin from the passenger. 'There's no point in ringing that number,' said Alf, 'I'm the owner and I shall drive.'

The AEC was a big improvement on Alf's two Leylands. Capable of topping 30mph, it could leave the Hippo behind, for that was flat out at 21mph. Going downhill was another

Opposite: early days. These photos may have suffered a little from the ravages of time but they do offer a fascinating glimpse into the past. A.B. Sutton & Sons, emblazoned on the cart, was the trading name used by the company right up to the late 1940s when the fleet of 44 vehicles was acquired by the Road Haulage Executive in the lead-up to nationalization. The initials were those of Alice Beatrice, but it was her youngest son, Alfred, seen here with the firm's earliest mode of transport in about 1925 after delivering to houses at Lea Green Station, who rejuvenated her ailing coal business. Alfred drew his coal from Lea Green colliery: when the pit closed in the 1960s, he bought the land and in 1989 it accommodates the operations of the Sutton International tank container business. Opposite below: the first goods-carrying motor lorry run by Suttons was a Leyland Hippo rigid six-wheeler registered DJ 5152. Rated as having a 10/12-ton carrying capacity, the vehicle was rather heavy for the era, weighing in at 7 tons 4 cwt unladen. Ex-Army Transport Ltd was the name of the business run by Soly Royal who provided traffic to Suttons on a subcontract basis. Alf Sutton is pictured with the vehicle in about 1932 outside his brother's garage at Marshall's Cross. Below: 'Oh Boy' may have been an expression that Alf Sutton uttered when he saw his brand new eight-wheeler in about 1937 although the name also followed on from that given to his Leyland Hippo, 'Big Boy'. Those who follow the AEC marque will identify the cab as being the type made by Oswald Tillotson, rather than by AEC themselves. AEC were the first non-steamer manufacturers to put a rigid eight into production in late 1933 or early 1934. The detailed attention to the paintwork is exemplified by coachlines on the front spring hangers, whilst anyone of note in haulage circles naturally put 'London' on the vehicle as its prime destination.

matter, for 'throwing the stick out' – freewheeling in neutral – would allow a rather hairy 60mph, if you were brave enough. Alf said that he couldn't slow down because the force of the rushing air underneath the vehicle lifted the floorboards and jammed the pedals.

A.B. Sutton & Sons entered the war running three lorries and came out of it operating twelve after buying up the vehicles of McKinnels of Irlam. But Alf saw the winds of nationalization starting to blow. 'I'm not going to work for the socialists,' he announced and immediately set out and bought a Nuffield dealership and garage on Prescott Road, saying he was going to sell cars for a living. Few people believed him, especially after he had bought the assorted 33-strong vehicle fleet of Richard Pilkington who wanted to get out of transport even quicker than Alf. The dozen Vulcan tippers amongst these didn't work for Suttons long, as Alf eventually succumbed to the Government's overtures, picking up a good price for his 44 wagons in what was laughingly termed a 'voluntary acquisition'.

Sutton's standing as a transport man had been already spotted by the Government inspectorate who appointed him as manager of the local St Helens depot on Sherdley Road. The post wasn't taken lightly; going back on his original promise, he put all his efforts into managing what he felt was his own piece of the BRS organization. Assisted by his wife

The Atkinson eight-wheeled rigid was the Suttons standard flagship from the day they formed up again after denationalization in April 1954. Still to be used nearly 30 years later, the eight-legger was only ousted because of the greater operational acceptance of the maximum-weight artic. LDJ 866 was one of four similar eight-wheelers going into service in one batch during 1959. There would be a full load in weight on the back of the Atky, Suttons specializing in the carrying of rather dense materials like white zinc powder used during paint production.

When Sutton & Son (St Helens) Ltd was formed in April 1954, the company had no depot of its own and the office was housed in a Nuffield car dealership in Prescott Road, St Helens. They soon moved into premises next door to the Boar's Head, rented from the Greenhall brewery, then in 1957 the expansion of the fleet prompted them to move across the road to their current base of operations at Sutton Heath. The quickly extended concrete hard standing there meant that rather than being parked around on any spare land, the Sutton lorries could be properly accommodated, and on Sunday mornings there were resplendent lines of Atkinsons as far as the eye could see. Only a dozen can be seen in this 1960 photograph, but of particular interest are the fifth and ninth from the left: these are DDJ 271 and 272 which were bought new at the start of the post-nationalization Alf Sutton business.

Above: having the appearance of a tipper, NDJ 793 actually illustrates the first version of the Portolite semi-trailer, which could carry liquid in a large rubber bag tank. The sides of the semi-trailer – which could be dropped inwards to allow general cargo to be carried – were used in conjunction with a set of webbing harnesses to prevent undue movement of the fluid load. When emptied the bags, which were made by Marston Excelsior, were rolled up and stored in lockers under the belly of the semi-trailer. This particular vehicle carried two bags which allowed two entirely different types of liquid cargo to be hauled without any risk of contamination. As there was no space available under the semi-trailer for landing legs, uncoupling this outfit had to be done using a set of skids. Below: although Suttons patented the Portolite – an idea still in use today – they soon recognized that vehicles carrying liquid in bulk by more conventional means were in great demand. They currently operate more than a hundred roadgoing tankers, with approximately one tractor unit for every 1½ tank semi-trailers. They generally carry any type of cargo in liquid form, though six tankers of an entirely different type were put into operation in late 1986 specifically for the carriage of pressurized gas. LDJ 329 is one of a batch of eight identical tractor units with consecutive numbering which went into service in 1959. This Dyson trailer was a semi-experimental vehicle which utilized disc brakes on the bogie, remembered as not being entirely satisfactory.

Ada, he made that Northern depot into what was arguably the most profitable centre of the BRS chain and he was envied for it by most of his fellow managers. Greatest rivalry was with Ken Brown who ran Kentish Town in London, but it was friendly rivalry and the bond between these two men was to last nearly 40 years.

Politics can be a fickle affair and when the Conservatives came back into office, it was rumoured that BRS was to be totally denationalized. Alf made his plans and lined up twenty of his best drivers. An offer of fixed employment was quickly accepted when nothing definite could be established as to what fortunes they had if they stayed on with BRS. Sorting out a fleet of vehicles was a bit more difficult and crafty Sutton spent a great deal of time repairing what he thought he was going to be allowed to buy, only to see all the vehicles moved on to another depot at the eleventh hour, with a set of much more questionable vehicles appearing in their place.

Monday April 5, 1954, was a memorable day in the Suttons calendar. On the previous Friday, Alf and his new drivers had all resigned en bloc from BRS. The drivers had been instructed to congregate outside the Nuffield garage on Prescott Road. Once there, they were driven over to the BRS depot where Alf presented a cheque in payment for 18 vehicles; 16 of these were runners, one was bought for spares and the other was a small van as a runabout. In the main, the vehicles were Atkinson double-drive six-wheelers, although JTB 814 and JTF 14 are recalled as being both Maudslays, a four-wheeler and a six-wheeler respectively.

Alf had studied all the vehicles in the BRS empire long and hard, and found that the Atkinson seemed to stand up best. Being built just up the road at Walton-le-Dale, Preston, meant the makers were very accessible, too. Joining the 18, Alf had already bought DDJ 271 and 272, both brand new Atky eight-leggers. All the wagons were kitted out with new ropes and sheets and, whilst the nine night drivers went home for a rest, the nine day shunters loaded half of the Sutton fleet for London, and the famous Sutton trunk to the Metropolis was only hours away from starting.

Alf Sutton could be an impetuous man. Once he had decided to do something then it had to be done, even though it might end in disaster. He did have an office in St Helens to work from but the London base just didn't exist. Alf had persuaded his old Kentish Town rival Ken Brown to run the London operations but for three months they didn't have an office and use of the telephone, number Tideway 1021, was only borrowed. This had little effect on the Suttons plan as nine vehicles the first night and nine the second night headed south for London.

The night trunk driver was a highly respected man. His vehicle was loaded up for him by the day shunter and once in London he just jumped down and left it for the day shunter to unload, then pick up northward-bound traffic. Glass, newsprint, paint, timber board, all of these were staple Suttons traffic and 35 years on they still form a big percentage of what is carried today. Alf Sutton and his team prided themselves on the service they gave, never missing an overnight delivery, an attribute greatly appreciated by customers like ICI who offered them the chance of expanding the Sutton empire. New plans were being considered for Glasgow, could Suttons work them traffic over the border? 'Certainly,' Alf said, although some of his drivers refused point blank to do the Glasgow trunk, the prospect of the road over Shap was just too much for them.

No such protest came from Bill Griffiths, who loved the Glasgow run especially with his favoured Atkinson 'Chinese Six' FDJ 965. Leaving the Jungle Cafe on the top and past the clock, Bill regularly threw the stick out as they hurtled over the narrow bridge at the bottom knowing that southbound traffic would stop at the top and let them take full rip. This was the only assured way of getting up the other side – sitting in the passenger seat could be a hair-raising experience! The driver's mate was a statutory requirement in the 1950s when a drawbar trailer was being pulled. Alf soon appreciated the value of this extra load carrier. He had another trick, too, performed on virtually all his non-eight-leggers.

Prior to 1968, operator licensing was tightly controlled, each authorized vehicle having its own unladen weight. If you wanted to exceed this weight you had to apply to the Traffic Commissioners and sometimes they just refused point blank. Alf Sutton thought long and hard about his six-wheelers which were both strong and very heavy. Experimenting with one Atkinson, he first removed the heavy timber body, pulled out the chassis, refitted a longer, lightweight eight-wheeled chassis and topped it off with a lightweight aluminium body. By adding a second steering axle, along with a trailing axle at the rear instead of a double-drive bogie, the result was a rigid eight-wheeler which weighed empty the same as the earlier six-wheeler, but legally could carry 4 tons more payload.

These Suttons conversions of the mid 1950s became part of the local folklore and with a trailer hanging on the back almost 22 tons of payload was legal. The 'wagon and drag' outfits were run well into the 1980s, although Alf got into artics too, almost by accident at first. Buying the 17 vehicles of William Bros of Peterborough, he inherited a strange mixed batch; Commers, Internationals, Vulcans and also a Bedford artic. Bill Lewin, who had learnt his craft driving the Scammell Scarab artics on the railway (these three wheeled units being known for some reason as 'Yo-yos'), was asked to go down to Peterborough and drive this new fangled machine back to St Helens.

In the convoy, only Ernie Jones knew the cross-country route but as time passed Ernie said he wanted some shuteye, much to the annoyance of Pat McAbe and others who were keen to get home but didn't want to get lost in the dead of night. 'Give me two hours, then give me a shake,' was Ernie's instructions but once he had got off to sleep, Pat reached in and wound his watch on to read two hours fast. 'Wake up Ernie,' Pat called. 'Well, it hardly feels as though I've had 10 minutes,' he replied, but looking at his watch he realized it was time for the off.

Back in Lancashire, the new artic was loaded up with glass bottles as Bill extolled its manoeuvrability compared

It was fitting that the major celebrations involving the production and sale of the 10,000th chassis made by Atkinson vehicles involved a four-wheeled tractive unit that was bought by Suttons. In the ceremony which took place in 1964, Alf Sutton, on the left with the scissors, stood next to Mr Francis Caunt, the Managing Director of Atkinson Vehicles Ltd. Fleet number 550 was to receive the registration XDJ 58, being uprated to run at 30 tons train weight after the laws on weights were redrafted in 1965.

Although very few people could imagine an early 1960s Atkinson fitted with anything but a Gardner engine, representations by Cummins for fitment of their engine into the Atkinson chassis prompted some head-to-head comparisons. Suttons agreed to furnish two-year-old SDJ 44 for the hill climbing part of the trials which took place in May 1964. Used for all the Atkinson climbing tests, Parbold Hill is ¾ mile long with an average gradient of 1 in 12. Observing fair play on the semi-trailer are Fred Millington and Barry McAbe. Although no results are known for this particular test, a similar T746XA tractive unit – the predecessor to the famous Borderer range – tested two years earlier took 5 minutes 24 seconds to clear the hill.

Alf Sutton's belief in the system of fitting a tank barrel into a frame the size of a standard container was to revolutionize the international carriage of liquids in bulk and also the work pattern of Suttons themselves. Under the title of Sutton International, the company now has in use in excess of 500 similar tank containers. Pictured at the Sutton Heath depot about 1972, this Atkinson-Dyson outfit is in the shadow of a massive clock tower that was moved brick by brick to St Helens about 1962. The clock, which dates from 1812, came from the estate of Sir John Whitmore at Ossett Hall. The motto on the other side of the tower reads 'There is a tide in the affairs of men'.

Today it is ERF which has the lion's share of the 200+ road fleet although Seddon Atkinson units still make a strong contribution to daily operations. The favoured Gardner engines of old have also been replaced by Cummins power packs. E909 ULV, here showing off the striking Sutton union jack livery on the A1 motorway at Bradbury, was one of a batch of curtainsider units put into operation on a particular glassfibre contract.

with the clumsy rigid and trailer. 'You can even drop the trailer fully loaded,' he told Alf and reached under to pull on a lever. What Bill had forgotten to do was to unwind the trailer legs because, doing all his work on the little Scammell, he was used to the automatic coupling on that vehicle which dropped the trailer onto a set of little wheels. The lever he pulled he thought had been the trailer handbrake, and with an almighty crash he demonstrated how to split the tractor and trailer and dropped all the bottles on the ground.

This incident apart, Alf soon identified the boon of articulation and so the fleet was destined to change its composition, even though he couldn't put one of his beloved trailers on behind an artic. A change in the make of tractor unit was also attempted briefly, with Sutton being involved in the formation of TVW (Transport Vehicles Warrington Ltd). The business started about 1958 after Alf and Tom Ward had become worldwide agents for the supply of Sentinel spares, following the closure of this company's road vehicle building operations. Together with Aaron Henshall, Oliver Hart and Ron Mason, the men bought the old tannery at Warrington where they went about building these rather special machines. It is recalled that only about 22 vehicles were built, all different from each other, and five of them went to Suttons. HDJ 124 was a four-wheeled rigid and HDJ 126 a six-wheeled rigid, whilst the others were four-wheeled tractive units. They are remembered as being good motors, but had difficulty in stopping. The normal engine was the Rootes two-stroke, particularly spiteful in being able to blow its exhaust manifold off, though in fairness this only happened because Tom Ward had fitted an experimental exhaust brake which did not have the desired effect.

Alf Sutton also got involved in other major diversifications. He bought a coal mine, a lead mine and even a brick works, although he wasn't aware that a kiln needed special lighting techniques. 'Pour some old sump oil in the top,' he instructed, hoping that would get the fire going, but all he succeeded in doing was to blow the top off the kiln with a mighty explosion.

A more successful scheme was the Sutton concept of the Portolite, a big rubber balloon with a hole in the top and an outlet valve on the side. The bag was used to carry bulk liquids inside a dropsider body that had the appearance of a tipper. Once the liquid was discharged and the bag rolled up, the sides on the trailer could be dropped and general cargo carried. It was a brilliant idea, patented by Alf, which is still in limited use today, but normally carried inside a 20ft container, which gives more stability than the drop-side artic. It was to be in containers that Suttons were to expand dramatically: not the normal type which has totally changed the handling of most international traffic, but tank containers, the small tank being mounted in what would be the space inside the container, supported by a large container-sized framework.

Suttons had got themselves into tanker work almost by chance. The Portolite experiment gave Alf a taste of liquid and when Andrews of Aintree had what should have been a Co-op road tank up for disposal, Alf took it and fitted it onto HMB 132, a rebuilt Atkinson eight-from-six-wheeler. First run carrying benzene, it reportedly stank like the devil, and it was transferred onto calcium as Suttons expanded their business base.

During the 1950s and '60s the Sutton empire had grown strongly. What had started in 1954 with a dedicated Liverpool-London service had first spread to Glasgow, then Newcastle, Durham, Billingham. Initially these were night services, but in specialist traffics like liquids, the day roamers crept into the dedicated Sutton structure.

Also coming into the Sutton organization was Michael Sutton, who joined the company in 1967 at the age of 19. Working first as a fitter, then in welding, he was also to learn the craft of electrician before going into the traffic office as a clerk and then into operations. By 1973 Michael had shown his father he had earned the right to be given a directorship. In 1977 he was responsible for initiating a striking change in the image of the company.

The Queen's Jubilee year saw a varied programme of events as the Monarch visited many parts of her homeland, and places so favoured were even to include St Helens. Michael found out the intended route of the progress and decided to plant one of the company's latest artics close by, carrying a large banner saying 'Welcome to St Helens'. In patriotic style, he painted the front of the red vehicle in the fashion of the Union Flag so when the Queen passed she couldn't miss seeing it. The Suttons staff stood on the trailer getting a good view and it was apparent by Her Majesty's look at the Suttons vehicle that the new paint job met with Royal approval. Since then, all the Suttons fleet have been painted the same way, a trademark now well known throughout the country.

The Suttons organization that approaches the 1990s is one that is firmly based on what Alf Sutton devised and strove for. Alf died after a short illness on Sunday, August 9, 1987 at the age of 80. Michael Sutton, who had been Managing Director since 1978, was at the helm of a company which now runs over 200 goods vehicles, divided equally between road haulage/distribution and roadgoing tankers. Warehousing at St Helens, Warrington, London, and Leicester is kept extremely busy, whilst 500+ tank containers operate worldwide under the name of Sutton International. Contract hire and truck rental is an expanding area, and Suttons still run a number of car dealerships which started in 1946 with that garage in Prescott Road.

The secret of Suttons may well have had something to do with the flair and imagination of Alf Sutton, a man who seemed to be a natural innovator. He combined this with very hard work by both himself and his team of workers, a winning formula that has been adopted by the next generation of the Sutton family.

5: W.A. Glendinning Ltd

Though not perhaps showing as high a profile as Suttons, the North-east-based concern of W.A. Glendinning Ltd also epitomizes the theme of the family haulage business. Now into their third generation and under the day-to-day control of directors Ken and Gordon, the company is named after Chairman and Managing Director, William Archibald Glendinning, called Archie by all who know and respect him. But it was Archie's father, George Edward Glendinning, who had steered his family into the haulage business in the early years.

Local coal deliveries by horse and cart to the houses of Shotley Bridge, near Consett, was the rather low-key beginning, with a variation during the summer when passengers were hauled, rather than sacks, out to local beauty spots at Stanhope and Blanchland. The one problem with Shotley Bridge is that it is situated in a deep valley and apart from the route 'down to the Town' – the city of Newcastle – all other destinations mean climbing at least one mountainous incline. Anything up to ten horses were used to head up those Sunday outings, although even then the passengers knew that for some of the way they would have to walk rather than be carried up the steepest hills.

As business developed, three horses were working out of the flour mill at Shotley. Then, in 1925, Glendinnings entered the motor age with the purchase of their first Ford motor lorry. The new 1-tonner cost £130 and was even fitted with an early tipper body. A chain-drive Sunbeam was run for a short time too, and not only did it double as both a flat and a tipper, passengers were also hauled by fitting temporary seats. In 1934, Glendinning was to buy the land which is still the site of their current head office. The land was bought from the late Captain Martell, RN, and trees had to be hacked back to gain access. With the River Derwent on the eastern side and a smaller tributary down the western side, the plot had the shape of an island, so Island Garage was the obvious name for the new base.

During the wartime years the Glendinning lorries were seconded onto airfield construction work and by 1948, eight tippers were being operated. Ex-army Bedfords, two Austins and an American GMC were in the line-up and amongst their drivers were two other sons of George – Ernie and Jackie – although both were to leave and set up on their own account in the early 1950s as Archie took over the reins and set about developing the business on his father's foundations.

Because of the local nature of the tipper work, which still embraced coal but also covered lime spreading, the threat of nationalization never came to Island Garage. But with the subsequent change of politics allowing more freedom in transport, Archie decided to have a go at long-distance general haulage work. Being rather strapped for cash, he had to adopt a novel way to get his first platform multi-wheeler. GFS 998 was a 1937 'Chinese Six' Albion that had originally pulled a drawbar trailer on its delivery pattern for the Newcastle Brewery. Archie saw the fine-looking vehicle at a dealer's yard in Benfield Road and traded in his Austin Sheerline saloon car in exchange for it.

John Thompson was soon given charge of what became the fleet flagship, albeit a rather mature one. Capable of hauling a 13-ton payload, the six-wheeler had a very fit Albion engine under the bonnet but was endowed with an awful braking system. The brakes were worked via a system of long rods and although they were adjustable, it was almost impossible to set them right. If you adjusted them when the Albion was empty, once a load was placed on its back the arching chassis meant the rods were stretched and the brakes applied before the vehicle even moved. Obviously, then, to ensure motion, the brakes had to be set up with the vehicle fully loaded, but of course when running empty the converse applied and there was very little in the way of stopping power at all.

It wasn't brakes, though, which worried John on his first

Once his business was firmly established, Archie Glendinning's favoured buys were to be from the Leyland stable, the Comet being considered a premium vehicle in the four-wheeled tipper market in the early 1950s. Most of these had the conventional bonneted shape, similar in appearance to Dodge four-wheelers of the period. When the forward-control cab was offered on the Comet, the great demand created an occasional shortage as a result of which specials like HTY 369 were produced, this vehicle dating from 1954. The tipper was one of two similar Homalloy-cabbed vehicles run by the operator. But both cabs were simply to rot and drop off after a few years, and they were replaced by Leyland-made cabs with the 'mouth-organ' front.

Seen at the top of Devil's Drop on the road between Shotley Bridge and Blanchland, HUP 992 has just left the Glendinning production line ready for some hard tipping work. Archie bought this 1947 Leyland from Durham County Council: they had run it as a four-wheeled Beaver and Les Bell added the second steering axle, the conversion to 'Chinese Six' meaning the gross weight of the vehicle was raised by about six tons. This was well within the capacity of the original Leyland 600 engine.

43

NTY 50 was also a 'Chinese Six' but this was a true Leyland Steer and at the time was the only flat run out of the Island Garage on long distance tramping. John Thompson was number one driver, a true ambassador for his company and the vehicle. From Falmouth to Thurso, Consett steel was hauled out and any type of traffic accepted to run back homewards. With a 600 engine coupled to a direct-top five-speed gearbox, top whack was a noisy 35mph. The vehicle was to be converted into an eight-wheeler with the addition of a Mammoth Major trailing axle before being worked to its death and subsequent cutting up. The Steer is seen here in the works of Vickers Armstrong about 1959.

For sheer size and character the Glendinning AEC wrecker took the fleet biscuit. It was normally referred to as 'the Matador' but AEC purists would say it was probably an 0854, which had a Matador front end linked to a Marshal double-drive bogie. It usually ran on general trade plates but because it was much in demand for snow plough duties, it was subsequently to be registered PTY 99. An AEC 7.7-litre engine coupled to a four-speed gearbox, high and low speed auxiliary box and four or six-wheel drive gave it an exceedingly slow gait. But for doggedness and reliability, the AEC was a champion.

long-distance haul carrying soap powder down to Nottingham, but a simple matter of the restrictions on the 'B' carriers' licence saying the vehicle was limited to within a 25-mile radius of its base, which at that point was about 150 miles further north. The police officer wasn't impressed with the 'natural country' type of approach put on by John, who had Bobby Bainbridge with him, and he was booked.

But John was a true ambassador both for his company and his profession as a lorry driver, and by 1958, he was rewarded with a brand new vehicle, NTY 50, yet another 'Chinese Six' platform. This one was to have an open 'A' licence which meant John ran as far afield as Cornwall and Caithness, usually carrying steel produced by Consett Iron Company. The Leyland Steer had a tremendous heart – and full air brakes – its 600 engine being well on top of the job required. Only once can John recall having to use crawler bottom gear in real anger, although the infamous Porlock Hill's 1-in-3 gradient has beaten many another goods-carrying vehicle in its life.

The carriers' licence for the Steer had been bought as Archie expanded his fleet by buying smaller operations, predominantly in the tipping game. The vehicles that came with the licences were normally Bedford or BMC (Austin/Morris), but when new ones were ordered Archie tended to specify Leylands which, he felt, were the finest ever to be made. Tippers abounded in the North-east of England due to the number of coal mines and stone quarries, and Glendinnings led the trend for multi-wheeler tippers with Steers, Octopuses and Albion Caledonian load carriers.

One vehicle that never officially carried a load was their AEC wrecker, an awe-inspiring vehicle just to look at, never mind drive. Archie had gone to the RAF surplus sales at Ruddington with Basil Minnigan where there were a few similar bowser type tankers for sale, but the one they bought was something special for it had fully floating rear axles. Archie was even approached to sell it back to the RAF, such was the interest it created, although back up at home it was welcomed more like a monster. Once the 2,500-gallon tank was taken off, in its place went twin-boom wrecking gear of Holmes manufacture obtained from an ex-WD Diamond T and the vehicle was ready for work.

On the road the 6x6 AEC was remarkably slow. It had the relatively small 7.7-litre engine coupled to a four-speed gearbox plus a high-and-low auxiliary box. The other main lever was to engage the front-wheel drive. But what the vehicle lacked in cold power it made up for in sheer heart. Bobby Bainbridge seemed to know how to get the best from the AEC. Its quickly acquired reputation meant the wrecker was in great demand not only in accident cases and snow-plough work for Northumberland Council, but also just to double-head lesser-powered lorries up some of the steeper northern hills. Stories are told of how Bobby would hang on and hang on as the AEC seemed on its last gasp yet still surmount the incline. The engine would drop almost to stalling but snatching back into 6x6 drive seemed to give it just enough extra beat to make all the difference.

For size, the AEC almost filled the Island Garage yard

but for sheer ingenuity Glendinnings' first artic was the real head-turner. In 1959, car transporters were still a bit of a rarity but Archie had the foresight to see growth in the demand for cars to be delivered with no mileage on the clock. Although Carrimores were leading the way in this field with their double-deck semi-trailers, the excessive waiting list meant Archie opted for a Taskers semi-trailer, its two fixed decks having the cars raised and lowered individually by a Burtonwood tail-lift. Heading up the trailer was SJR 100, a BMC tractor unit rated as a 12-tonner for artic operation. John Thompson, leading fleet driver on the sole tramping vehicle, NTY 50, was asked to take on the new transporter which initially brought new Fords and Vauxhalls back to their respective local dealers in Consett.

Soon, the idea of having a locally based transporter concern caught the imagination of other North-east main dealers, and winning a contract to serve the large Morris concern, Buists, meant that new transporters came thick and fast. The contract vehicles were painted in the blue colour scheme of Buists. The paintwork, including sign-writing, like that on all the fleet vehicles, had been the domain of Bob Grindle. Bob had started out with Archie a long time back as a driver and began sign-writing on a part-time basis. After a day's driving he would take a vehicle door home with him and overnight it would be adorned with the Glendinning name. With the fleet expanding quickly, Bob was soon doing the painting full-time although the pressure was sometimes a bit difficult to stand. Looking out of the window one day, Archie's secretary, Nancy, noticed Bob miss out one of the many letter Ns in the Glendinning name.

UBB 623 dates from 1954 and up until 1960 was operated by British Paints, the Octopus hauling a four-wheeled drawbar trailer for most of its early life on long-distance tinned paint distribution work. Glendinnings bought several such second-hand Octopuses for tipper work, all being magnificently painted by ex-driver Bob Grindle. Tommy Vickers was this vehicle's first driver and, not being used to such a long body, had 40 tons of ore dropped on its back when running out of Tyne dock. The subframe couldn't lift the tipper body and the excess had to be hand-shovelled off. Behind the Leyland is the crumbling 'Chinese Six' Albion that had started Archie out on his long-distance work.

Glendinning transporter men will recall XOM 70, built new for Avon Car Transporters of Solihull, as the work-horse of their Kidlington depot. Avon had one life out of the Austin four-wheeler and drag, then Glendinnings used it as a ferrying vehicle to draw three or four new cars out of the factory at a time and relay them to the company's holding depot. The sloper bodywork was built by Alastair Carter when he worked at Abelsons prior to setting up on his own account in transporter construction. Once a year, the 1959 four-wheeler would make the long journey north to Shotley Bridge so that it could be rejuvenated for another hard twelve months' work.

Nancy hadn't the heart to interrupt the hard-worked Grindle and a later approach, though diplomatic, still prompted a furious uproar in frustration.

The increase in transporter work prompted the opening of a small staging depot at Kidlington, just north of Oxford, to hold the cars which were drawn out of the factory on a daily basis. The northern-based vehicles could thus collect a load any day of the week. With CJR 320B, Glendinnings had a vehicle that could carry nearly twice as many cars as anyone else. A Leyland Super Comet hauled a four-wheeled drawbar trailer, each having Carrimore superstructure, and although theoretically limited to speeds 10mph less than a normal heavy, the 'wagon and drag' was

still doing three return trips a week between Newcastle and Oxford for, strong head winds apart, she was a flyer.

Into the mid 1960s, Archie's two sons Ken and Gordon were realizing that they had diesel in their veins and finding ways of giving vent to their natural interest in transport. Ken served his apprenticeship at Consett Iron Company but at weekends he was normally doing a run down to Kidlington and back for a load of cars. A strange anomaly in the law meant that as their first transporter tractor unit had an unladen weight of only 2½ tons, it wasn't classed as an HGV so someone under the age of 21 was allowed to drive it. As soon as he finished this apprenticeship Ken came onto the driving staff and made the Super Comet 'wagon and

Bought specifically to work on contract to the North-East Vauxhall Bedford dealer Adams & Gibbon, this TK Bedford transporter was recalled as being quite a flying machine. The Leyland 400 engine producing 125bhp worked through a Clark overdrive-top gearbox and Eaton two-speed axle. Albert Shaw was the vehicle's first regular driver, its bread-run being between Luton and Newcastle. The semi-trailer was of Harvey manufacture, its upper deck being raised by threaded screws rather than hydraulic rams. The Bedford was to suffer a twisted chassis after rolling over in Wales, its impressive transmission then being transplanted into a BMC tipper.

A view of the Island Garage yard about 1970 reflects the dominance of both tippers and Leyland/Albion vehicles at that time in the fleet. TJR 290 is an Albion Reiver whilst UJR 419H is also a tipper but on a Lynx chassis. Perhaps the most famous vehicle in the fleet is the next in line, UJR 420H, another Lynx but converted into a six-wheeler with a Primrose rear steer axle. Its claim to fame is that it is the only Glendinning vehicle to have gone abroad when director Ken Glendinning used it to take a rhino to Southern Ireland. Next to that is SJR 59, a four-wheeled Comet which is beside RJR 871, an Albion Clydesdale tipper. The last two in line are a Badger tractive unit and a six-wheeled Reiver.

drag' his own for three years. The long legs of the 400 engine coupled to a six-speed overdrive-top Albion gearbox and Eaton two-speed axle meant a gear ratio for all seasons. The performance was marred only by a chassis which had steel suspension that could lean trememdously on the turn or with a brisk side wind. Ken only stopped driving the transporter full-time after he fell off the top deck when loading in Coventry, the two days he spent in hospital with a dislocated elbow made bearable only by regular visits from the local female car-delivery drivers.

Back at work, it was to be his fitting expertise that was needed, as the fleet suffered like many others with problems over reliability and lack of spares for the Leyland engines. Archie had vowed in the distant past that he would never have a Gardner engine in the yard but in the search for reliable service he had to go back on his word as ERF and Atkinson chassis powered first by Gardner and then by Cummins took over from Leyland. This applied not only to the general haulage/tipper vehicles, as the car transporters also had premium traction. But the trailers they were hauling were set to change in an exciting fashion. In conjunction with Allan Cooper of Carrimore, Ken Glendinning came up with the idea of the CVC. Not only could it carry cars and vans – its first two initials – but also cargo, as the top deck of the double-deck car carrier was made to fall flat and allow for loads of steel to be carried in a southerly direction and so cut back on what was normally 250 miles of empty running.

About eight CVCs were put into service, and it was only the attitude of the car transporter drivers' union that put paid to their dual purpose. Glendinnings were told that their vehicles were either car carriers or general haulage vehicles, they had to be one or the other, they couldn't be both. As the main part of the CVC's role was to carry wheeled vehicles this was the task they stuck to until a decision by the car manufacturers hit the haulier in a way they couldn't react to.

What happened was a major change in how a car gets from the works to the garage. It had always been the responsibility of the buying dealers to arrange transport. In line with the new vogue set by car importers, it was now decided to make it the responsibility of the car maker to arrange for delivery. The makers in turn decided to offer

Although the company currently operate a Crusader tractor unit for shunting duties, Scammell vehicles just hardly existed in Glendinnings history, 158 WBB being the sole exception. It too started life with British Paints in 1963 and on coming to Shotley Bridge was run as a platform vehicle on general haulage. It came to grief one day when Norman Edgar loaded it with long steel plate out of Consett Iron Company. It had only reached the A1 at Durham, 12 miles away, when the whipping created by the excess overhang of trailing steel twisted the rear of the Scammell chassis. The trailing axle eight-legger, powered by a Gardner 6LX 150 engine, was straightened before going onto tipper duties.

Opposite, above: the impressive old AEC six-wheeler was eventually put out to grass, but the Holmes twin-boom recovery equipment from it – which had originally come off a Diamond T – was transferred to DVT 723J, the company's current recovery vehicle. This ERF was bought by its first owner in anticipation of an increase in the permissible weight of an artic provided a double-drive six-wheeled tractive unit was being used; before coming to Shotley Bridge about 1975, it was used to haul clay from Devon to the Potteries. Glendinnings originally used it to haul loaded trailers out of the Hownsgill Plate Mill, the infamous steep exit beating many a conventional artic unit. Powered by the Cummins 250 engine, with a Fuller nine-speed gearbox and Kirkstall rear axle on a Hendrickson bogie, it has proved to have extremely good traction when on recovery work.

contracts to those hauliers big enough to take a whole slice of the country as their delivering region: as Glendinnings weren't large enough to tender for this type of work, it meant they were pushed out of carrying cars for British Leyland. They were to be the last of the small independents running out of Oxford – but as this door closed, another one opened

virtually on the company's doorstep.

Nissan, who were to commence importing their vehicles through Teesport, went against the trend in offering big delivery contracts and preferred to use smaller operators for individual loads. Glendinnings were on hand to take cars from their first boat and currently this type of work keeps a

Having experienced trouble over spares, support and sheer unreliability with the Leyland engines, Glendinnings went over to a Gardner allegiance in either ERF or Seddon Atkinson chassis. HRG 60N is recalled as being the first B-series ERF to come to north-west Durham. Ken Glendinning is seen here preparing to unload his cargo of coal which he had brought to Crookhall from a colliery in Northumberland. The tipper was fitted with an Anthony Carrimore alloy body, Gardner 180 engine, Fuller nine-speed gearbox and Kirkstall hub-reduction axles, and is remembered as doing very well for the company, being sold down in East Anglia when Glendinnings came out of tipper work in the early 1980s.

lot of their modern-day transporters very busy.

The wind of change was set to blow quite drastically in other ways through the town of Consett and although many, including myself, thought it would never happen, the early 1980s saw British Steel close forever the Consett Iron Company plant. Glendinnings didn't have a large amount of traffic out of the plant but what the closure did mean was that far too many tippers were chasing after far too little traffic. Such a formula meant tipper rates in the area fell dramatically to such a point that Glendinnings decided to quit and sold off all their tipping vehicles.

Archie Glendinning seems to have a considerable gift of foresight, for five years earlier he had taken over a transport depot at Pity Me, close to the A1 near Durham City, to cut down the dead mileage between the base at Consett and the booming area of the region on Teesside. The drop in vehicle numbers was soon compensated for, with the sold tippers being replaced by long-length steel carriers and more artics for general haulage work.

The Pity Me base, under the control of Gordon Glendinning, now heads up the general haulage arm of the company, the 24 vehicles based there carrying cargos like steel, cable and plastic piping as the mainstay of their work. All the car transporter outfits are based at Shotley Bridge although very few of the company's vehicles get back to base during the week as all the Glendinning fleet roam the country wide. One slight distinction between the two halves of the fleet is that the car transporters are painted with a band of blue round their centre, an addition to the colour scheme prompted once again by the transporter unions who decreed this so they could tell if the general haulage vehicles were being used on car delivery work.

It is not generally realized that Glendinnings have been involved in transporter work for 30 years. Archie fought long and hard through the channels of the Road Haulage Association in many ways that prompted changes in the law. His efforts were recognized when the RHA awarded him life membership in December 1987, a fitting honour for someone who strived for the highest professional standards, a cause being carried on by the family who follow him.

50

Opposite: Glendinnings have received excellent service from their ERF vehicles and continue to use them for all aspects of their traffic, not least of which is car transporter work. This E10 tractor unit has the 290bhp version of the Cummins L10 engine, so there is at least 10bhp per ton available to a vehicle that has been down-plated to 29 tons train weight. Kenny Robinson from Blackhill is at the helm of the ERF, punching south on the A19 at Crathorne. The semi-trailer is one of four similar Hoynor tri-deckers that can usually carry nine vehicles of most sizes or up to 12 Minis. Having the Cabstar pick-up perched at the rear in this instance limits the height of the centre deck thus preventing the ninth vehicle being slipped in underneath.

Fleet List
W. A. GLENDINNING LTD

ERF vehicles

No	Reg no	Chassis no	Type*	Engine	Model
112	VNL 178T	37666	T	NH250	38C2TR
143	YVK 220V	41255	T	NT240	38C2TR
141	YVK 221V	41042	T	NT240	38C2TR
107	ATN 806V	43118	T	NT240	38C2TR
114	ATN 807V	43121	T	NT240	38C2TR
116	DFT 520W	43234	T	NT240	38C2TR
118	DFT 530W	43238	T	NT240	38C2TR
115	DFT 512W	43071	T	NT240	40C2TR
140	CGR 792W	30627/2	T	NT240	38C2TR
117	TCX 890X	46726	T	NT250	C36
130	RNY 649Y	46967	T	6LXCT	C36
113	RNY 652Y	47041	T	6LXCT	C36
126	FYB 442Y	46887	T	NT250	C36
129	FYC 420Y	46872	T	NT250	C36
124	A405 LCX	48919	T	6LXCT	C26
134	A406 LCX	48951	T	6LXCT	C26
138	A407 LCX	48940	T	6LXCT	C26
149	A644 JHD	48269	T	6LXCT	C36
151	A476 PYB	48416	T	NT250	C36
146	B609 OEH	50541	T	LTA10/290	CP40
147	B995 OFA	51003	T	LTA10/290	CP40
152	D451 HWS	55937	T	LTA10/290	E10
142	E712 YMA	55916	T	LTA10/290	E10
127	E77 DVK	57757	R	6BTA	E6
144	E78 DVK	58643	T	LTA10/290	E10
150	E79 DVK	58648	T	LTA10/290	E10
145	E980 FJR	58379	R	LTA10/290	E10**
108	F871 KBB	59456	T 6x2	LTAA10/325	E10
125	F835 LCU	61575	T	LTAA10/325	E10
153	F169 LVK	61815	R	6BTA	E6
154	F	62531	R	LTA10/290	E10**
148	F	63080	T	LTAA10/325	E10
119	DVT 723J	18913	R 6x4	NHF240	66CU***

*Type: T, artic tractor unit; R, rigid
**drawbar   ***recovery

Seddon Atkinson vehicles

No	Reg no	Chassis no	Type*	Engine	Model
120	JNL 181X	73308	T	NT250	401
105	RCN 667Y	74206	T	NTE290	401
131	VBB 702Y	75812	T	L10/250	301
122	A40 AVK	76676	T	L10/250	301
109	A979 BTN	76831	T	L10/250	301
121	A516 ANL	77281	T 6x2	L10A/290	301
137	D406 WNL	81248	R	Perkins Phaser 180	211
128	F198 JBB	85458	T	L10A/290	311
104	F830 LJR	85782	T	LTAA10/325	Stratos

*Type: T, artic tractor unit; R, rigid

Mercedes-Benz vehicles

No	Reg no	Chassis no	Engine	Model
110	MVK 163X	385028-2-4-622561	OM401	1619 4x2
132	KJR 292X	385028-2-4-601911	OM401	1619 4x2
133	MFT 231X	602367 28 216 661	OM616	307D van
101	A926 GEF	602318 20 608 409	OM616	307D
102	C457 VAJ	602318 20 705 814	OM616	307D
103	F608 SAJ	602318 20 903 106	OM616	307D
123	F613 SAJ	25 396 571		814
136	F635 RVN	617131 25 374 113	OM422	16/255

Various vehicles

No	Reg no	Chassis no	Type*	Engine	Model
139	E313 NDC	314184	T	310	DAF 95-310
106	PCX 310M	WHV 52819	T	RR 280	Scammell Crusader
111	F973 HGS	JA97229	T	L10A/290	Ford Cargo 38/28
135	B526 WYA	2CFA189000 2350 363	R	Fiat 140	Iveco 109-14
155	F443 VDC		T	Cat 3306B	Foden 4400

*Type: T, artic tractor Unit; R, rigid

51

6: Knowles (Transport) Ltd and Wisbech Roadways Ltd

Whilst both Suttons and Glendinnings proudly emblazon their name on their non-contracted revenue-earning vehicles, one other long-established concern has deliberately avoided putting the family name on half of the fleet's vehicles. The colour schemes of both Knowles Transport and Wisbech Roadways are a very similar, prominent and distinctive red and white, but the Knowles family reckon they have detected that some of Wisbech's customers prefer to deal with that particular haulier precisely because it does not have an obvious family name linked to it.

Wisbech Roadways was founded in 1958 by the late Gerald Knowles. At that time his famous Knowles Transport concern, of Wimblington, had already been in business for over 25 years. Knowles trace their origins in transport back to 1932 when, as a 17-year-old, young Gerald scraped together £75 as payment for his first vehicle, a second-hand Ford Model T. Knowles had never really shone in his schooling but what he wasn't afraid of was hard work and since the age of 13 he had laboured on the farms round Chatteris, about 15 miles east of Peterborough. The flat agricultural land of the region has long been producing vegetables for the rest of the country's markets. Carrots might be Chatteris' greatest claim to fame but Knowles was involved in moving all sorts of other traffic up to and beyond the 1½-2 tons that the Model T would normally carry. Even fitted with solid tyres on the back end, the T didn't really like this overloading abuse and within a year Knowles had traded the vehicle in for a heavier A-type Ford.

1933 also saw the arrival of the licensing system many thought of at the time as a restrictive practice to try and curb the power of the road haulier when compared to the railways. Because Knowles was already in business he was immediately granted a 'B' carriers' licence although this was soon upped to an open 'A' licence with freedom to carry goods anywhere. Knowles was also issued with a driver's log book in which he was supposed to record rigorously all the hours he worked, these too being restricted by the newly imposed laws. He didn't take much notice of his new record book and recalled later that he put it under his seat for five years before someone asked for it. The innocent response from the fresh-faced Knowles meant very little punishment was received for this lengthy omission.

In 1934 Knowles traded his Ford in for his first Bedford, a second-hand 4-tonner registered EG 8487. Bedfords were to stay a Knowles favourite for nearly 40 years although within two years Gerald was to swap this first one for a machine which was to see him right through the war. On paper the vehicle might have been known as a 3-tonner but Knowles adopted what was a standard rule of thumb for uprating its capacity by simply calling it a 6-tonner. No visit to the testing station, no expensive paperwork, just a state of mind, in the days when overloading for most operators was almost a way of life. The vehicle was later uprated to a 10-tonner with the addition of a third, trailing axle but this was done in a professional manner by Scammell & Nephew of Spitalfields, London. Knowles recalled paying £315 for this Bedford and, working the beet, both driver and machine were severely tested.

In this area of the country, sugar beet is almost a way of life. Between September and January the beets are clawed from the ground and hauled up to feed the insatiable demand of the sugar factories. In general, Knowles tended to shuttle between the fields and the railhead, but the last load of the night was trunked into Peterborough before the factory closed at 10pm. No fancy loading equipment in the 1930s: it was back breaking shovelling both on to the back of the wagon and then off at the other end.

Knowles' greatest invention, to his mind, was his own modification to a basic garden fork which he made wider and stronger to fork the beets. He also forged his relationship with his wife, Florence, who was to work alongside her husband in the family's business right up till his untimely death in 1988. Flo may not have had Gerald's physical strength but she could carry the Tilley lamp into the field and she provided inspiration and comfort through those long dark nights as the beets were hewed from the frozen ground.

Another Bedford was run alongside the 10-tonner in the late 1930s but that was seconded for wartime use and Gerald was left with just his own six-wheeler to haul the war years away, restrictions on petrol coupons permitting. By 1946, the hard work of the previous 14 years was to pay off. Frugal attention to costs, which included coasting down any decline he encountered to save on petrol, meant Knowles could afford the exorbitant going rate of £1,000 a vehicle when he wanted to increase his fleet. He was really paying for the coveted carriers' licence but hardly had he got his fleet of half-a-dozen vehicles together when the wrath of the law makers came down on the transport men again with the compulsory purchase of the fleet in nationalization.

Not naturally a hard man at heart, Knowles fought both hard and long when the valuation team came to

Doddington. Letters from the BRS solicitors, Swallow, Swallow & Crick, came thick and fast but in Gerald's own brief, Sandy Green, they met their match, and the eventual agreed price was three times what had originally been on offer, plus legal costs. Knowles received the cheque in payment one day in 1951 and the next day he was to buy four brand new Bedford four-wheelers and a 10-ton artic, all consecutively numbered KEW 140, 1, 2, 3, 4. True, he wasn't allowed to run them on general haulage, but moving bricks for the Whittlesey Brick Co on a 'C' hiring licence meant that for the next three years the Knowles transport interests were kept ticking over.

Gerald spent his spare time converting his bungalow at Doddington into a petrol filling station. Then in 1954, with the promise of denationalization, he placed his bids for specific lots of vehicles which were up for disposal by the Road Haulage Executive. Not knowing how many bids would be successful, he went rash and tendered for about 100 vehicles at the March, Whittlesey and Kings Lynn depots. He bought them all but what might have been acute financial embarrassment didn't occur for there were many

Looking back more than 30 years, this O-series Bedford may seen rather dated but in about 1955 this scene represented a high degree of modern innovation in handling sugar beets. John McKinnon is at the wheel of the Fordson-based tractor loader whilst looking on is Charlie Chandler, driver of the Bedford and brother-in-law to the late Gerald Knowles. In the cab is Tony Knowles who was destined to take over the reins of his father's company. Particularly of note, leaning against the grille of the Bedford is Gerald Knowles' own version of the beet loading fork which he developed from a standard agricultural manure fork.

Knowles ran two Rutland six-wheelers during the mid-1950s and they were recalled by Gerald Knowles as being among the fastest goods vehicles on the road at that time. Fitted with the AEC 7.7-litre engine and an Eaton two-speed axle, the 4½-ton unladen weight six-wheelers were capable of reaching 70mph on the flat, a fairly hairy potential at a time when speed limits for this class of vehicle were less than half that. One drawback to the lightning performance was that the wheels, which were fitted using eight studs, had a habit of coming off. Knowles were later to remedy this stud shearing by bracing each with four separate strips of metal.

owner-drivers wanting to take these extra vehicles off Knowles' hands, not in lots but one vehicle at a time.

Even after selling some of the vehicles on, Knowles still had about 50 to his name, far too many for the picturesque village of Doddington to stand so, after receiving some persuading comments from the Council, Knowles moved down the road to custom-built premises at Wimblington, the current home for the family concern. The traffic of the 1950s varied between bricks and timber, with agricultural loads as the fleet's backbone, the platform four-wheelers being converted with sideboards to make them suitable for the hectic beet season.

Although this pattern of working had been his formula since he had entered transport, Gerald sensed he was missing out on something. Wisbech may have been only 10 or 15 miles down the road, but the Knowles company was based too far out to be regarded as a local haulier. Hence the missed opportunities: for what differentiated Wisbech from any other market town in the area was the River Nene and the fact that its depth and width allowed fairly big vessels to treat this place as a port. In 1958, Knowles got his chance when Norman Bush decided to sell up his fleet of about 20 vehicles as an ongoing concern. The vehicles may not have been in the best condition but working first out of rented

The purpose built depot constructed at Wimblington was a big improvement on the cramped facilities and grass verges used at Doddington. Part of the fleet lined up here in 1956 shows the variety of vehicles then in use by Knowles. The big S-type Bedford four-wheelers were favoured for agricultural use but for heavier, long-distance work, Fodens were preferred. The second Knowles Rutland is the third vehicle from the right, parked beside an AEC Majestic 'Chinese Six' bought second-hand from Scottish haulier Peter McCallum. Taking centre stage is Knowles' QL Bedford recovery vehicle: they bought this ex-MoD vehicle from a local vegetable merchant who had used it to haul carrots from the muddy fields to the washery. Knowles fitted the Harvey Frost 5-ton crane and were to use the vehicle for a further 20 years.

HJE 322 originally came to Wimblington as a demonstrator vehicle, Foden allowing Knowles to have two weeks use of what was their latest S20 eight-legger. So impressed was Gerald Knowles with the 1958 vehicle that when the Foden representative came back to retrieve the vehicle, Gerald told him that he wanted to buy it, paying cash for it there and then. Fitted with the rather leisurely Gardner 6LW 112bhp engine, the vehicle is remembered for its stopping power – air brakes on the Foden were a big improvement over their normal engine-generated booster brakes.

premises and then converting an orchard into a large depot, Knowles, under the guise of Wisbech Roadways, was able to open wide the doors of this potential business. Meeting the needs of agriculture and shipping may have both had their own drawbacks, but putting them together meant a far wider base for the fleet.

For cargo carriers Knowles remained faithful to the Bedfords as his mainstay, and the big S-types were replaced by the TKs. But for heavier work, the Foden-Gardner combination became unsurpassed among the eight-wheelers although there was also a sprinkling of AECs, ERFs and Leylands.

In true family tradition, the two Knowles sons, Gerald (Junior) and Tony, entered the business, and whilst things followed a steady course for about ten years, the events of 1969 were to have a major effect on the Knowles operations. What started out as a disagreement over pay and conditions blew up into a blistering 13-week strike that was to leave scars on both sides of the union fence. The only vehicles running were driven by the two Knowles sons and even they felt the wrath of the picketing strikers, Tony still bearing the marks of a brick through the Foden windscreen.

Seen on the day it was delivered new to Wimblington in 1962, NJE 949 shares the photograph with owner Gerald Knowles and his two sons Gerald junior (right) and Tony (left). Tony Knowles was to learn his craft on this Gardner 6LX-powered vehicle, acting as a trailer mate when the eight-wheeler was coupled to a four-wheeled drawbar trailer. The young Knowles also gained experience of a rather unlawful nature when occasionally occupying the seat fitted on the offside of this vehicle, before coming of age.

During the 1970s, as a diversification in their traffic flow, Knowles served East Anglia with a great deal of container work through Manchester Liners. Although the fully loaded boxes were carried south-east on maximum-capacity vehicles, Knowles tended to run the empty boxes back to Manchester on a smaller four-wheeler. Gerald Knowles (junior) is at the wheel of the Volvo power-loader whilst NCE 344H is one of four similar AEC Mercurys run at a time when the company also had a large number of AEC Marshal six-wheeled tippers.

What the damaging strike did achieve was to make Knowles reconsider their whole transport strategy. Never again was Gerald Knowles going to depend so much on so many vehicles: the idea of phasing out the smaller four-wheelers and only running maximum-weight outfits was to become Knowles' philosophy as the company made bulk haulage its business. Emptying a ship of 2 or 3,000 tons of steel might otherwise have meant hiring many hauliers but Knowles were to make jobs like this their own, not through buying lots more vehicles but with increased numbers of semi-trailers. The hard-working tractors could simply shuttle backwards and forwards to their huge storage depot on the outskirts of town. Whilst the ship could be unloaded as quick as they wished, the loads could be delivered out into the country at a more leisurely pace. Agriculture too was set to change its working practices as co-operatives, bulk buying and bulk selling meant traffic more in line with what

Knowles were now ready to offer.

In 1983, whilst many companies pondered at length over how they should enter the 38-tonnes field, Knowles didn't falter. They carefully considered both the 2+3 and the 3+2 combinations and were to quickly discount them for the 3+3 configuration. True, a six-axled outfit wasn't mandatory, but the freedom from worry over axle loads or king-pin placement more than compensated for a slight drop in potential payload. What is slightly different in the Knowles outfits is that they tend to opt for a very close, 1.1-metre axle spacing on their tri-axle semi-trailers. This does drop about 2 tonnes off the bogie's capacity but it doesn't really matter with a three-axle tractor unit. What the closeness of axles does give is far longer tyre wear as it cuts down the scrub of this hard-working rubber.

So the company of the late 1980s places a total emphasis on maximum-weight outfits. A couple of double-drive

Not as swift across the ground as the flighty Mercury, the Gardner 5LW-powered ERF 54G four-wheeled rigids nevertheless gave Knowles good service. Good service also from driver John Fitzjohn, seen in the cab of OJE 456J, who has now clocked up more than 20 years with the company. There would be 10 tons of bagged potatoes on the back of the aluminium body, destined for market delivery stretching to places as far apart as Covent Garden, Gateshead and Glasgow.

Opposite, above: Knowles were to remain faithful to Bedfords from their early days in the 1930s up until the KM range of the late 1960s. Mechanically, the engines of those KM vehicles turned out to be a nightmare. Preceding the KM range, the TK Bedford had been the first fully forward-control cab, this in turn having followed the snub-nosed S-type Bedford. To give his drivers more protection in the event of an accident, Gerald Knowles devised a system of double bumpers and Bedford were so impressed with the idea that they incorporated it into the KM range, although Knowles never received the acknowledgement he felt he deserved in coming up with this concept. Seen leaving Whittlesey near Peterborough, this KM is hauling bricks supported on a Scammell-built 'Fourtrak' four-in-line semi-trailer.

Although owning the company of Wisbech Roadways since its formation in the late 1950s, Knowles have always run the two firms as separate entities albeit on a co-operating basis. They currently share similar red and white livery to their parent company although that is the only outward sign to denote ownership. This trio of Leylands are seen at Wisbech quay receiving fertilizer in bulk, a type of traffic which is now a company speciality. Wisbech found the Marathons, pictured first and third in line here, to be far better machines than the Buffalo in the centre.

eight-wheeled tippers are the only rigids retained for special application, the joy of articulation meaning that flats, tippers or curtainsiders can be used to carry the cargo as required, with specialist coil-carriers and long-length trailers available as well. The Knowles fleet is based on premium vehicles with both Volvo and Scania the current family favourites, although Foden, ERF and Leyland have been well used and are highly thought of. A special sector of Volvo F7s belies the three-year replacement plan, for these units are on dedicated local work, hardly doing 300 miles a week.

They tend to haul empty tin cans into the storage area of Wisbech, or other traffic destined to be moved further inland by the fleet's 38-tonners.

Taking the bulges of arriving ships and seasonal agriculture in their stride has meant that Knowles have developed heavily into warehousing both at Wimblington and Wisbech. That aspect of transportation can both be more lucrative and give you less heartache than running trucks – but there seems no sign that the Knowles family will ever leave what has become their life blood.

With the introduction of the 38-tonnes weight band in 1983 for five-axle artics, many operators pondered on whether to run a 2+3 or a 3+2 combination to incorporate the extra axle. Knowles quickly assessed the various alternatives and chose instead the 3+3 six-axled outfit, one more axle than the law actually requires, and faith in their decision has augured well for the running of their operations. It would also give them a boost with the legalization of 40 tonnes on six axles in the UK. The 6x2 ERF looks a finely balanced machine but along with Foden and the Leyland/Scammell six-wheelers they have all lost out in favour of Volvo and Scania units, preferred by Knowles because of better service support.

7: Hallett Silbermann Ltd

Describing Hallett Silbermann as specialists may not be strictly accurate for they readily turn their hand to a wide range of transport problems, far wider than most general hauliers. But it is heavy haulage that the company started out with and their current fleet specializes in moving anything up to 80 tons in weight. Another perhaps less well known speciality of the company is that a number of the vehicles which are liveried in Hallett Silbermann's red and white colours are in fact being operated by owner-drivers who work on exclusive contract to the company.

John Silbermann, chairman of the Brent Group of Companies Ltd, which embraces amongst its many diverse interests the operations of Hallett Silbermann Ltd, has long put his faith in subcontractors, ever since the days of Peterson Ltd, the trading name of his first clearing house business, which he established in September 1946. That company was to specialize in finding low-loaders in the days when lorries of any type were both in short supply and in great demand. John had learnt of the uses of this heavy haulage tool when he had gone straight from school to work for C.E.A.C. Howard in Bedfordshire during the Second World War. Howards ran about five ERF 20-tonners. But John's second employer, Coupar Transport of Acton, was mainly a clearing house, albeit relying principally on heavy haulage traffic.

John left his employ at Coupars in a ridiculous fashion. A complaint he made about drivers talking in the office while he was on the telephone to customers just got out of hand, and a full-blown argument with his boss over the matter made him threaten to leave if he wasn't given better consideration. John was promptly shown where the door was and in a fit of pique he walked out.

But the young man didn't regret it. The next three months of extended holiday was spoilt only by telephone calls to his flat from customers of Coupars complaining that John was the only one who knew what their needs were and

they couldn't get any sense out of his old employer any more. John suddenly realized he had something to offer the transport world that people wanted and instead of being employed in a traffic office at no more than £4 a week, why didn't he set up on his own account?

So in September 1946, Peterson Ltd went into the clearing house business, the only signifigance of the adopted name being that Silbermann thought it would be one that was easily remembered by operators and customers alike. The office premises were in East Finchley and although Peterson had very close relationships with established heavy hauliers like Frank Annis, they tended to favour owner-drivers like Tom Hallett, a man who had been in haulage since finishing soldiering in the 1914-18 war.

In 1951, the clearing house traffic was so busy that a move of office to Cricklewood was prompted. Tom Hallett approached John around that time and said that he was thinking of retiring and, as they had a very close relationship, he gave John the first opportunity to buy his bonneted Dodge low-loader. The Dodge may have been old but what it did have was an open 'A' carriers' licence, which, in the days of tightly controlled licensing, meant that you were almost in an exclusive club. Heavy haulage was one of the sectors of transport which had escaped compulsory nationalization, so John sensed that this was a chance which he couldn't turn down. To ensure the transfer was done correctly, Tom Hallett agreed to set up as a limited company – T.Hallett Ltd – the sole assets to the business being the Dodge low-loader and its licence. In 1953 Silbermann bought the company of T. Hallett Ltd for the sum of £750 along with its goodwill, its vehicle and licence, the first acquisition for a fleet that was to grow to an eventual peak only one short of the magic 100 vehicles mark.

In the days of the total dominance of both British Rail and British Road Services, it was deemed to be a monumental occasion when John was able to get authority to increase his

As a company, Peterson Ltd began trading in September 1946, the name of his clearing-house firm being plucked out of the air by John Silbermann in the belief that people would remember it in the future. In those early days, Laings would require a moderate amount of traffic to be moved, in the region of four to six jobs per month. This mobile cement mixer, believed to be part of a concrete batching plant, weighed in around the 3-ton mark and was made by Benford who are still in business, based at Warwick. FDF 675 dates from 1946, and is the Dodge low-loader run by Tom Hallett in Peterson's colours and sold to John Silbermann when Hallett decided to retire. The vehicle had a licence weight of 2 tons 10 cwt.

With Peterson's clearing-house business getting bigger and bigger, it even merited having a British Road Service contract vehicle painted in their colours. The arrangement was to last for about four years, between 1949 and 1953, the period when BRS had almost exclusive rights in transport under a rigorous policy of nationalization. The ERF DMJ 856 dates from 1944, and is here carrying John Mowlem's plant number 72, a rail-mounted crane of about 12 tons weight. Howard Nunnick's research suggests that the carrying capacity of the crane would hardly be any more than about 5 tons. It was probably originally steam powered but the lack of chimney suggests it may have been converted to diesel. Due to the need to negotiate sharp-radius rail curves, the wheelbase of the crane is quite short and it would probably have had to be jacked down or secured to the rails when lifting to give better stability.

carriers' licence by 100%, having an additional vehicle. In 1953, with a change back to Conservative politics, older vehicles and special 'A' licences were put up for tender and Silbermann successfully bought a Bedford, GYK 168, from Pickfords Tower Bridge Road depot and a 20-ton Foden, DGE 223, from Glasgow. Conscious of the possibility that a change back to a Labour government might see his new purchases re-acquired into BRS, John set up a new limited company called John Silbermann Ltd to own both vehicles and licenses.

In the mid-1950s, the going rate to buy licences was between £100 and £200 per ton of unladen weight, so naturally expansion was only slow. By 1958, the combined fleets of T. Hallett Ltd and John Silbermann Ltd, which ran in the same colours out of the same depot at Midland Brent Terrace, off the North Circular Road in London NW2, had grown to about ten in number. The Dodges, Bedfords and Fodens had all gone, their important licences transferred to Scammells. Most were fairly elderly machines, but in that year 977 RMD, a 40-ton box tractor, came new from Watford, with 136 VMC, a new 6x4 Junior Constructor following in 1959.

Although never capable of moving the really super heavyweights themselves, the clearing house approach

During the mid-1950s, Scammell low-loaders painted in identical colours but under the separate names of T. Hallett Ltd and John Silbermann Ltd were a regular sight in London Docks. In this scene, believed to be at King George V Dock, the Battersea lighter is being used as an intermediary between the deep-sea ship and the roadgoing low-loader. The Hallett artic dates from 1939, whilst the Silbermann Scammell EXT 939 is a 1938 version of the Watford-built tractor. To personalize the vehicles before fleet numbering, Silbermann vehicles were named 'Red' somthing, 'Rooster' in this case, Hallett vehicles 'Green' something. George Baker's research shows that Silbermann bought four second-hand Scammells that were former Shell Mex artics in this period.

Scammell first began producing their rigid six-wheelers as early as 1926, Robert Wynn being one of the many operators who used this type of machine as an overnight trunk vehicle up to London. The stores department of the GPO had a total of eight of these six-wheelers either in box van or platform guise. George Baker traces GGH 253 as one of two that Silbermann bought, these being chassis numbers 2842 and 2843. Dating from December 1939, the vehicle's unladen weight is 6ton 7cwt 57lbs, in the days when six-leggers could only gross 18 tons. Being on contract to Mallett, Porter & Dowd Ltd of Kings Cross, London, the Scammell was unlikely ever to be overloaded as its main cargo was waste paper, cloth & woollens. Silbermann ran this contract for about eight years.

Above: at the time it came into the Silbermann fleet, KKX 629 already had a chequered career behind it but also a lot of heavy hauling in front of it as the fleet flagship. On November 22, 1944 it had been delivered new to the Ministry of Supply, George Baker recording that its model code of RP15 denotes it as a 30-ton capacity tank transporter. The Pioneer chassis, number 5630, powered by a Gardner 6LW engine, left Scammells' coupled to tank-carrying semi-trailer number 2859. It was sold out of Government ownership on September 9, 1947. Pictured here on the North Circular road at Hendon it is hauling a Dyson float 60-ton capacity drawbar trailer carrying a 37RB excavator base machine weighing in at about 40 tons. All-up combination weight is close to 80 tons. Below: Silbermann's old Pioneer was to be pensioned off on the arrival of 136 VMC. The 6x4 Junior constructor was popular with Pickfords in ballast tractor form but John Silbermann ordered his vehicle for use as an artic tractor unit. George Baker notes that chassis number 10340 was also special in that it was the first Scammell to be fitted with the Gardner 6LX 150bhp engine. Delivered to Silbermanns on April 30, 1959, it is pictured here in the works of Ransome & Rapier at Ipswich in February 1967. The brand new machine being carried is an NCK 605 which weighs around 50 tons and the lack of A-frame and boom suggests it was en route to London docks for export.

adopted by the Silbermann companies meant that they never refused to quote for any job they were asked about. One of the oddest was to move a 107ft-long pole from London Docks to Windsor Great Park and John Silbermann still recalls querying the reasoning of his colleague Stan Wiles who quoted only £25 for the task. 'The publicity will do us good,' said Stan, though tackling the job wasn't to prove troublefree despite a relatively low weight of only 12½ tons.

The pole was a gift to the Queen from the people of

British Columbia, having been hand-carved from a 600-year-old Western Red Cedar tree by Chief Mungo Martin of the Kwakiutl tribe. Putting a value on such a load made the insurers go dizzy but protection from foam blankets where the pole was supported on the bogie bolsters helped the night-time haul through the Metropolis to pass without incident. If you go into the Park today, a plaque beside the pole will tell you that it was erected into place by the Royal Engineers. This isn't really true, for although they did assist, it was Silbermann's man John Jelly who organized the twin

As an area of diversification, John Silbermann set up a company called Metroplant which, as its name suggests, specialized in hiring out plant throughout London. The big advantage in having plant mounted permananty on a vehicle was that the law then didn't class the plant as being a load, thus the vehicle could be operated without a carriers licence as it was classed as either a motor tractor or a locomotive, depending on its travelling weight. 180 MPK dates from 1959 and is one of three Thames Traders which were operated for only a relatively short period, reflecting what the company felt about these new Fords. Grossing about 9 tons, the vehicle-mounted air compressor was hired out to road constructors and builders for concrete breaking.

John Silbermann found that if he could prove a 'new demand' for vehicles then the licensing authority would be prepared to grant new carriers licences to meet that particular traffic. 7100 MM, which dates from 1962, was one of the new breed of fleet vehicles – a long way from heavy haulage – bought to fill distribution contracts linked to storage of a particular product on behalf of its manufacturer. The Commer was one of three similar vehicles fitted with the Rootes two-stroke engine, carrying up to about 4 tons of cargo. Although distribution was throughout the UK as the map suggests, the company specialized in south-east England including London and the Home Counties.

pulley mechanisms to ensure the pole was put up in the same pristine condition that it left Canada.

The heavy haulage brigade, due to the dramatic nature of their day-to-day traffic, had a way of grabbing public attention and people stood amazed that these long, wide, high or heavy loads could reach their destinations by road unscathed. The late driver Bill Upham, however, had a particular way of drawing extra attention to himself which meant that even broad-minded John Silbermann had eventually to dispense with his services. He took a terrific

pride in his Scammell, and the Gardner engine was kept so clean that it gleamed in the light. The awful trick that Bill got up to, when driving across, say, the infamous Hanger Lane junction in West London with a long load, was to stop his outfit in the middle as he feigned an engine problem. With the traffic stacking up around him, he would lift the side panels on the Scammell bonnet and show off his gleaming engine as everyone watched him. Just before people reached bursting point, Bill would announce that he had fixed the fault, climb aboard and then slowly power the Scammell

On March 13, 1964, John Silbermann bought out Styring Transport Ltd and absorbed it as a wholly owned subsidiary into the Brent Group of Companies Ltd. This was done specifically to establish a base in Yorkshire which also ran A-licensed vehicles. Styring only had a small fleet, about six vehicles, but operating artic tippers in the early 1960s was something of an innovation. The 1962 Super Comet would be fitted with the 375 engine and was used at local civil engineering works and for material supplies. The semi-trailer shown is an example of George Neville's famous 'Dumptrailer', renowned for its exceptionally low centre of gravity. The landing legs fitted here were detachable.

Hallett Silbermann were to move a great deal of contractors plant around although this NCK Andes crawler crane would hardly test the Volvo F89-Taskers combination as the load only weighed about 40 tons. SMJ 292R was a Hatfield-based vehicle owned by the company, its regular pilot being Bill 'Ginger' Howell, who at the time was top driver at Hatfield and a big friendly rival of Hornchurch-based John Macklin. The Andes was a popular crawling machine, often used with a drilling attachment for bored piling. NCK named all their machines after mountain ranges like Pennine and Atlas or individual mountains like Eiger and Olympus.

Opposite: in July 1977 Hallett Silbermann were involved in this movement of components which were to form part of a power station, hauled from Mere in Wiltshire and bound for Cowes in the Isle of Wight via Southampton docks. Leading driver of the company, John Macklin, was sent to supervise the convoy which consisted of five similar vehicles. With an overall diameter of 17 feet, these sections were made more difficult to handle by the multitude of small lugs springing from the exterior. Pictured slowly leaving Mere, the leading Volvo F86 was driven by David Langworthy who is flying the flag to celebrate Jubilee Year.

away, confident that no one would forget seeing him and his resplendent Gardner engine.

As well as the heavy haulage and clearing house businesses, John Silbermann was also deeply involved in plant hire around London under the name of Metroplant Ltd. He also identified the need for warehousing and distribution, decades before the concept became fashionable. In 1963, he set up a 45,000 sq ft warehouse at Feltham in Middlesex and distributed everything from paint to jam round the shops of London on behalf of the products' manufacturers. In the following eight years, this arm of the Silbermann business was to run up to 30 vehicles and employ 100 clerical, warehousing and driving staff. In 1971 it was sold as a complete business unit to Carryfast Ltd who were themselves developing this type of distribution business throughout the UK.

Silbermann meanwhile was busy buying other companies, their vehicles and a chain of strategically placed depots. In the early 1960s the 11 vehicles of Grove Garage, Edgware were acquired, whilst the six vehicles of Styring Transport Ltd also brought with them a depot in Wickersely, Rotherham in March 1964. Reeves Transport Ltd in Acocks Green, Birmingham was bought in 1971 which assured a Midlands foothold and three years later the famous London name of Cattermoles was acquired. Most recently, Jacques Transport of Watford has been added.

The passage of time also saw John lose his concerns over any prospect of re-nationalization, so in 1963 the two names of T. Hallett and John Silbermann were joined together into Hallett Silbermann Ltd, the current banner used for haulage operations. Main base of the fleet is the Hatfield depot situated on Travellers Lane in Welham Green, under the day-to-day management of Jon Hugill, with the whole Hallett Silbermann company now under the control of MD Alan Hampton. Hatfield is also the base for the company's international operation.

It was in 1957 that Silbermann was first asked to quote for international work when a shipping agent asked them for a price to move a 22-ton diesel engine generator from Switzerland to ICI on Teesside. '£500,' said John, not really knowing what he had let himself in for, but the job was his. Liaising with a Belgian haulier to tow the Silbermann trailer whilst it was on the Continental leg of the journey, John and his wife spent five days sorting out a route and checking on bridge heights to make sure the passage of the load went like clockwork. 'Let me know when the load's delivered,' came the call from the shipping agent just over a week later. John told him that it had already been craned off at Middlesbrough and the low-loader was back in the garage. 'Can you do 11 more, one every three weeks?' was the next request, and since then the Silbermann vehicles have travelled as far afield as Russia, Portugal, Scandanavia and the Middle East, including Israel.

That Continental influence has now spread into the vehicle line-up too, both for national and international operation. The Scammell dominance of 30 years ago has changed as DAF, Volvo and Scania are now more in favour both with Silbermanns and their owner-drivers. This trend away from a totally British-originated fleet of vehicles is also reflected in part by our next specialized carrier.

```
Fleet List
HALLETT SILBERMANN LTD

Vehicles based at Hatfield

Fleet no   Reg no      Make and type
W128       C599 DBW    Volvo F7
W129       C619 FOV    DAF 2100
W130       C851 HUK    DAF 2100
W131       C425 JNK    DAF 2100
W132       A399 JBW    DAF 3300 6x4
W133       E86  YBM    DAF 2800
W134       E976 CKX    Volvo FL6
W135       E977 CKX    Volvo FL6
W116       XMT 359T    Shunting tractor
           C910 HVS    Ford Transit
WOD32      DVS 312T    ERF 'B' Series 40C2
WOD34      D519 MON    DAF 2100
WOD39      A404 GMY    DAF 3300
WOD40      D280 OBW    Volvo F12 6x4
WOD44      Q171 VME    Volvo F12 6x4
WOD45      B220 YBW    DAF 3300 6x2
WOD46      B363 WHY    DAF 3300 6x2
WOD47      EGT 456X    Ford Cargo 1513
WOD48      B192 UFC    Volvo F7
WOD49      BYC 400X    Volvo F10
WOD50      C463 LBE    Volvo F10

European vehicle fleet

Fleet no   Reg no      Make and type
EOD3       C536 EMD    Volvo F12 Globetrotter
EOD4       C538 EMD    Volvo F12 Globetrotter
EOD9       VRT 232X    Scania 142M
EOD12      C537 EMD    Volvo F12 Globetrotter
EOD16      PJX 161X    DAF 2800
EOD17      D689 HMK    Volvo F12
EOD18      B843 XOO    Volvo F10 6x2
EOD19      C425 GUS    Scania 142 4x2
EOD20      YPU 147X    Leyland Roadtrain 4x2
           OVS 666W    DAF 2800

Rotherham vehicle fleet

Fleet no   Reg no      Make and type
R357       C810 KWE    Leyland Roadtrain
R358       B663 CDA    DAF 2100
ROD8       D943 PAK    Volvo F10
ROD11      EJL 561V    Volvo F12
ROD14      B953 AGJ    MAN 20/321
ROD24      WNW 755X    Volvo F12 6x4
ROD26      DFP  69Y    Mercedes 20.28 6x2
ROD27      UCH 822X    DAF 2800 6x4
ROD28      MUA  49V    Scania 111 4x2

Birmingham vehicle fleet

Fleet no   Reg no      Make and type
B544       LOV 257X    Bedford TK
B549       C615 FOV    DAF 2100
B550       C423 JOJ    DAF 2100
B551       C935 HVS    Ford Fiesta
B552       D524 MON    DAF 2100
B553       D858 PDA    Ford Transit
B554       E933 SOC    DAF 1900
B555       E758 TOJ    Ford Transit
BOD3       C622 FOV    DAF 2100
BOD4       HKV 496V    DAF 2100
BOD5       C623 FOV    DAF 2100

Leicester vehicle fleet

Fleet no   Reg no      Make and type
LOD4       STN 598S    Scania 111 6x2
LOD5       UPT 145V    Scania 6x4
LOD6       E862 BDM    Seddon Atkinson 4x2
```

8: Thomas Gibb (Fraserburgh) Ltd

Although Gibbs of Fraserburgh are not the largest fridge van operator around, their solid line up of 25 maximum-weight artics are perhaps one of the most pleasing sights on our roads. Their colours of red, white and deep navy blue could be dismissed as rather old fashioned amid the sleek, glitzy fashions of the late 1980s, but where Gibbs' resplendently turned-out vehicles shine is in giving a traditionally high standard of service in a business that they have been at a lot longer than most.

Gibbs have been running fridges for over 30 years and they can trace their roots back into traditional horse-and-cart haulage in the late 19th century. It was grandfather Jimmy's two sons Jimmy and Tommy Gibb who took the Gibbs haulage business into the motor age, but before the firm got too big to be reckoned with, Sutherlands of Peterhead came along, made the brothers an offer too good to refuse and bought out their business. Whilst Tommy Gibb returned to the family farm for a living, Jimmy stayed on in haulage as a manager for Sutherlands. When Sutherlands in turn were bought out by the Government during the period of nationalization in the late 1940s, the brothers got back together again to run five immaculate coaches on private hire passenger transport.

Running these Leyland Royal Tigers took the Gibbs name throughout the mainland of the UK. Then in 1953, when the restraints affecting road haulage were eased, Jimmy and Tommy sold the coaches on, bought a couple of Albions with their respective licences from BRS and went back into haulage. Expanding your fleet at this period was a slow business but by 1958 they had reached double figures and thought it good business sense to form a limited company. As Tommy had continued farming, it was Jimmy Gibb who had been the most involved in the haulage branch of the family businesses, and the brothers decided to call the new company 'Jimmy Gibb (Fraserburgh) Ltd'. But a check with Companies House revealed there was already a limited company called Jimmy Gibb based in Edinburgh. To prevent any confusion, Tommy Gibb's name was substituted and that is the company title still in use today.

The concern is currently directed by another combination of Tommy and James Gibb, today's two brothers being sons and nephews to the earlier pair. They both joined the company as it started to expand in the late 1950s, Tommy Gibb cutting his teeth on the little Albions and S-type Bedfords that used to predominate in the fleet at that time. The largest vehicles in use then were a 'Chinese Six' AEC Majestic and a mouth-organ fronted Leyland Octopus eight-legger. Apart from a bonneted Ford Thames 4D four-wheeled tipper which ran locally with coal, sand and gravel, the rest of the fleet were on long distance work. Paper from the mills at Aberdeen was regular cargo destined for London and timber from the local Scottish forests was another frequent Gibbs burden. But since they were based in a fishing port, it was almost inevitably fish that Gibbs relied on as their staple traffic.

Following the fishing fleets round the coasts of Britain meant that the Scottish lorry drivers were real wanderers. It also made for more interesting lorry spotting because it wasn't unknown for Fraserburgh-sourced vehicles to be based three and four hundred miles down country for several months of the year as the fishing boats worked out of places like Whitby and Lowestoft.

Fish was sold at differing prices depending on whether it was classified as fresh fish or fish intended for freezing and for later processing. As rates for the latter type were only about half the price of fresh fish, it was decreed that fish sold to be frozen had to be loaded directly onto a refrigerated vehicle rather than onto a normal platform lorry. This Government order prompted a flurry in container buying by some fish men; prior to this lawful instruction fridge vans for fish work were virtually unknown.

Gibbs, though, didn't rush into fridge van buying. The

Jimmy Gibb started his haulage business off in Fraserburgh with one horse in 1896, added a second horse the following year and, by the time this photograph was taken at the turn of the century, had an established carting concern in the Scottish fishing port. The herring season was a particularly busy time for the Gibbs carts, working the boxed fish from the quayside up to the curing yards, taking the fish offal on to the surrounding farms for manure and back-loading from there with peat. During the winter the carts were used to haul road-making materials out from the town. Despite the rather time-worn condition of this photograph it is evident that the pristine condition of their vehicles was already a Gibbs trademark – as it still is 90 years on – this example apparently having won an award at a local show. Gibb himself, seated next to his wife Elizabeth in the centre of the cart, survived until 1935, weighing 22 stone at the time of his death.

cost at that time of about £2,500 apiece for an insulated container made it quite an expensive commitment and, weighing anything up to four tons empty, the containers meant a big erosion in potential payload. Against this, Gibbs did find their fridge vans would get the first loads when there was a queue of waiting vehicles, so there really was enough traffic outward bound for all the vans or boxes they had at their disposal. Keeping their options open, Gibbs bought at first removable containers for this fridge work, cooled by dry ice. This meant the vehicles were available for any other traffic – once the box was removed – but interchanging and varying the source of loads got to be such

a headache that Gibbs eventually specialized and went totally into fridge work.

The vehicle line-up of the late 1960s had changed greatly from the Albions and Bedfords of the '50s. AEC Marshalls and Atkinson six-wheelers both strengthened the fleet, although in essence the two types of vehicle were like chalk and cheese. Alastair Laird, now transport manager at Gibbs and related to the Gibbs family through marriage, recalls that his brand new Marshall of 1965 vintage was a real flyer for its day and could rattle on to a top whack of 55mph. In contrast, the Atky six-wheelers with Gardner 150 engines were pushed to reach 38mph flat out, although this slower

VSA 177 was the second Atkinson to join the Gibbs fleet, following a year after UAV 917 which came to Fraserburgh in 1960. Both had the Gardner 6LX 150bhp engine and although particularly powerful for a six-wheeler in the early 1960s, the Atky was only capable of a top speed of about 40mph. The fridge body, which was built by Gibbs, is held down by a set of chains onto a platform body also built in-house. The M-model Petter fridge has a single-cylinder BSA engine run on propane gas. The single-drive six-wheeler was first regularly driven by Andy May who can recall limping back from London with only half a cab after an accident badly damaged the front nearside of the Atky.

Following the accident to VSA 177, Gibbs decided to fit as standard a substantial crash bar to give more protection to the Atkinson glassfibre cab. When FSA 201D joined the fleet in 1966 it was one of only four Atkinsons and it joined a similar number of Leyland Comet four-wheelers: fleet predominance at that time was shouldered by AEC Mustang and Marshal six-wheelers. Intended for heavier going than normal, 'Outlaw' was fitted with a double-drive bogie, rear diff lock and Gardner 6LX 150 engine. Regular driver was James Scott, 'Little Scotty'. Although nothing is known about the fate of FSA, identical six-wheeler UAV 917 is still all in one piece but in prime condition for restoration being owned by a coalman near Peterhead.

Following the success with the Comets, Gibbs tried out a stronger Leyland Retriever, but GAV 100E is recalled as being something of a rogue vehicle. Mechanical faults included failed rear hub oil seals, burst radiators, fans and fan blades breaking and rust on the cab. Cylinder head gasket failure on the Leyland 600 engine meant the vehicle was regularly towed home. The Leyland had a number of drivers, William Watt, Jim Cowie and Alan Strachan, and, failures apart, they did report that the vehicle was capable of a top speed up and beyond 70mph. It was used to haul large paper reels south from Aberdeen before getting a fridge body, and turned over at Airdrie fully loaded with frozen raspberries before Gibbs thankfully disposed of it. The Leyland was still to get the last laugh on its first owners for, more than 20 years after this photograph was taken, 'The Conqueror' is still hard at work on the showman's circuit in north-east Scotland.

Above: by 1967 Gibbs were dipping their toes into the operation of maximum-weight artics; HSA 800F was recalled as being the first Gardner 180-engined vehicle to run in the north-east of Scotland. The vehicle's first driver was Eddie Thom. With a top speed capability of 50mph, the tractor unit is shown coupled to a Crane Freuhauf semi-trailer. This Jan Borowski photograph, taken on the beach promenade at Fraserburgh, shows 'The Clansman' loaded with canned goods from British Fish Canners. Below: with its interchangeable trailers the artic was a far more versatile combination than the rigid eight-legger. But where classic double-drive vehicles like 'The Pride of Scotland' were to score was in adverse weather conditions where traction, especially with a part loaded artic, could be a nightmare. The fridge van shown here was another Gibbs build. First regular driver was Andy May, known as 'Andy Capp', who recalled a top speed of 46mph from the six-speed David Brown gearbox and 150 Gardner engine.

With a premium being added for Gardner engine fitment, Gibbs were to try out the Cummins power-pack, more powerful on paper, for the early 1970s phase of Borderers. SSA 789K was recalled as the third Atkinson having the Cummins 205 engine and there were to be four or five tractors with the Cummins 220 engine. First driver of 'The Pathfinder' was Kenneth Stephen, known as 'Farmer', who reported the unassisted steering very stiff. With Fuller nine-speed gearbox and Seddon rear axle the vehicle tended to record 6 to 7mpg. Mechanically, it had a large number of problems, the rear axle oil seals and rear springs requiring attention every two months. The diff went in October 1973, the gearbox in May 1974 and it needed major engine attention in 1975. The Gray & Adams van body was cooled by a BMC 1100 engine run on gas driving a Petter PCL fridge unit. The Highway trailer chassis was a lightweight skeletal with the van secured by twistlocks.

This view of North Street, Fraserburgh in 1971 illustrates the Atkinson predominance in the Gibbs fleet at that time. The depot was actually an old herring curing yard where barrels were also made. Gibbs used it for storing both empty vans and also loaded fridges that could be driven off mains electricity. Seen in the background are the two lifting implements that Gibbs used for fridge box transfer: both the RL Bedford mobile and the hand-operated crane needed treating with a great deal of respect and many a grey hair resulted from their operation. NSA 111H in the foreground was a 6x2 Volvo F86 that was recalled as being good on power although trouble with all its bearings and rear suspension meant it was never really liked. The Transit pick-up in the centre was named 'The Busy Bee'.

rate was so steady that you could set your watch by them, their performance was that regular.

But the Marshalls didn't like sustained speed on the growing network of motorways, and running fish to places like Billingsgate in London meant a journey of 541 miles from Fraserburgh. Covering the same mileage on the way back, the fridge vans tended to carry foodstuffs for the Scottish naval bases on the west coast. Running over the dreaded 'Rest and Be Thankful' summit caused a terrific build-up heat in the AEC's gearboxes and Alastair Laird recalls that it wasn't unknown for individual gear wheels to be welded together.

With the fridge vans being more and more in demand, Gibbs increased their fleet's potential capacity not by a massive increase in vehicle numbers – Tommy Gibb is more than happy sticking round the 20 to 30 mark – but by going up to maximum-weight/capacity outfits. Eight-wheeled Atkinsons were tried, some even with an increase in their wheelbase, but Gibbs sensed the real way forward was in artics, with the Atkinson Borderer as their favoured workhorse. This famous type of Atky took the company into the 1970s, the Gardner engine, David Brown gearbox and Kirkstall axle combination covering millions of trouble-free miles delivering the frozen/chilled/cooled products on

Both the Seddon and the Seddon Atkinson tractive units did little to impress the Gibbs family. The late 1970s and early 1980s saw a total transition to resplendent ERF units (with the exception of a lone Sed Atky 401, 'The Prince of Scotland', WRS 971Y). Representative of the new ERF generation is 'The Highland Queen' seen here just south of Perth with driver Eddie Thom behind the wheel. Eddie is Gibbs longest serving driver having been with the company for 32 years. Gibbs followers will not find VRS 42Y listed in their old fleet lists: the registration mark on this photograph was doctored from VRS 42X so that an apparently more modern vehicle could appear in a contemporary ERF advertisement. The Crane Fruehauf semi-trailer van is cooled by a Petter PDL fridge.

ERF were to remain a Gibbs favourite but in the run up to the announcement of 38 tonnes in 1983 they were slow in offering a twin-steer tractive unit with a specification to suit the Gibbs requirements. Tommy Gibb decided to try A790 ESS, the name 'The Invader' indicating how the Dutch-built machine was invading UK territory. Regular driver was Stevie Pallo, a meticulous man who was soon converted to a 100% DAF advocate. Going into service in November 1983, it ran until August 1987 before it required its first major attention, that being a new clutch. A new set of injectors and a new alternator were fitted in mid-1988, although each year the front brakes had to be relined. Pallo returned a regular fuel consumption of 7½mpg running at 38 tonnes gross. This Geoff Milne photograph shows the vehicle near the Forth Bridge coupled to a Crane Fruehauf semi-trailer.

board. When they were in need of attention Jimmy Gibb (Junior) was back at base ready to carry out repairs, having learnt his craft from head fitter Bill Wright, or 'Diesel Dan' as he was affectionately known. To sense what was wrong with an engine, Bill would place his hand on the side of the block or cylinder head and, like a veterinary surgeon caressing a heaving flank, give his diagnosis from the feel of the vibrations.

When Atkinson and Seddon merged in the mid-1970s, the predominance of Atkinsons was set to change. The company were never as happy with the Seddon influence, though they tried their best with the new offerings. It was to be ERF tractor units that took their place right up until 1983, when the big decision about how to run at 38 tonnes was on every transport man's mind. Weight had never been a big problem with Gibbs, but they did have the potential headache of drive-axle overload in the period when the vehicle was running part laden. Tommy Gibb decided to opt for the three-axle tractor unit hauling either a tandem-axle or tri-axle semi-trailer van, but when ERF were asked to make a twin-steer tractor with the Gardner engine fitted they weren't very interested. They did offer such a unit with the Cummins or Rolls-Royce power pack but Gibbs in turn didn't really want that option.

As the haggling was going on, Tommy Gibb decided to try a DAF 3300 6x2 unit, and since that momentous occasion, more than 14 other Dutch-made six-wheelers have come to Fraserburgh. The subsequent ones were all the 2800 ATi version, Gibbs feeling that having the optional 16-speed gearbox fitted more than compensates for the nominal drop in power. The current mix of DAFs and ERFs haul a total of 30 different fridge vans, all capable of carrying either palleted traffic or hanging meat from the 130 double hooks fitted on 5 meat rails. The vans are cooled by a mixture of Petters, Thermo King and Carrier diesel-powered fridge units. These newer fridge vans are normally made by the fellow Fraserburgh business of Gray & Adams, being specified on air suspension to give a smoother ride which is very much appreciated for some of the more delicate traffic like fresh fruit.

For the last 10 years, Gibbs haven't carried any fresh fish:

they find it far less traumatic to source their outward-bound loads from a triangle bordered by Aberdeen, Buckie and Fraserburgh. Sixty per cent of this trade is still fish – the balance tending to be meat – but all processed or packaged in some way. The luxury of a single drop is also long past, for the Gibbs drivers have anything up to 26 drops to contend with, which sometimes stretch across the entire length or breadth of the UK mainland.

Many of these runs are to the same drops week in and week out as the demand for Scottish fish and meat is met with 'just in time' deliveries to butchers' shops and hotels throughout the country. To give a service 52 weeks of the year, the Gibbs drivers operate a strict rota of holidays so that even when other lorry drivers may be collectively thinking of national holiday breaks, especially at the turn of the year, the Gibbs men are still punching up and down the road. They are normally home just once a week, which means the drivers spend most of their time with their outfits, each worth close to £100,000. The distinction from other fridge vans on the road lies in the individual name hand-painted just below the windscreen. Evocative titles like 'Northern Star', 'Monarch of the Glen', 'Pride of Buchan' and 'The Clansman' may have little significance to the casual onlooker, but to the Gibbs man it personalizes the vehicle and it is a regular reminder of that distant home.

Fleet List
THOMAS GIBB (Fraserburgh) LTD

Reg no	Make and type	Name
A790 ESS	DAF 3300 6x2 artic	The Invader
A625 FSO	ERF 'C' 4x2 artic	The Thistle of Scotland
A290 GSS	DAF 2800 6x2 artic	The Avenger
A206 HSS	ERF 'C' 6x2 artic	Pride of Scotland
B799 JSS	ERF 'C' 4x2 artic	Pride O' The North
B130 LSS	DAF 2800 6x2 artic	The Crusader
B951 LSA	DAF 2800 6x2 artic	The Rampant Lion
B916 NSA	ERF 'C' 6x2 artic	Monarch Of The Glen
B279 JHH	Toyota 4-wheel pick-up	The Road Ranger
C707 OSS	DAF 2800 6x2 artic	The Clansman
C549 RSS	ERF 'C' 6x2 artic	The Conqueror
C550 RSS	ERF 'C' 6x2 artic	The Big Rig
C919 RSA	DAF 2800 Ati 6x2 artic	Northern Lights
C35 SRS	DAF 2800 Ati 6x2 artic	Bonnie Scotland
D161 VSA	DAF 2800 Ati 6x2 artic	The Scottish Soldier
D712 VSS	DAF 2800 Ati 6x2 artic	Highland Laddie
D115 WSS	ERF 'E' 6x2 artic	Hail Caledonia
D141 WSS	MAN 6x2 artic	Road Ranger
D979 WSS	DAF 2800 Ati 6x2 artic	Mull O' Kintyre
E818 ASA	DAF 2800 Ati 6x2 artic	Highland Rover
E477 BSA	DAF 2800 Ati 6x2 artic	Highland Queen
E353 BSS	DAF 2800 Ati 6x2 artic	The Highwayman
E171 CSO	DAF 2800 Ati 6x2 artic	The Highlander
E845 DRS	DAF 2800 Ati 6x2 artic	The Pathfinder
E848 DSS	DAF 95 6x2 artic	Clan Chief
F666 GSA	DAF 95 6x2 artic	Northern Star

9: Autocar & Transporters Ltd

The advances in more efficient methods of refrigeration and vehicle insulation are undoubtedly ensuring the job of the Gibbs driver has been made a lot easier. A similar leap in technology affecting another specialized operation, however, has meant far more headaches for its vehicle's driver. For in the field of car transportation, cramming the maximum number of fee-earning vehicles on board has become something of a daily puzzle. The trend towards stacking, decking-up and interlapping the cars on single, double or even triple-decked outfits is a necessity to ensure operations and movements are done in the most efficient manner possible.

Car transportation as a specialized haulage business is a relative infant in the world of carrying. The concept only really became viable in the late 1940s with the introduction of the first double-deck outfits. Subsequent expansion in the trade has seen many of the early pioneers merged or taken over and some have simply disappeared, but one long-established carrier still going strong is Autocar & Transporters Ltd who base their large national operation on the custom-built depot at Middle Lane, Wythall, on the southern fringe of Birmingham's outskirts. Autocar's current fleet is heading towards the 200 mark and, although they are short of their one-time peak of about 260 outfits, the more efficient modern transporter means that far more cargo can be hauled by far fewer vehicles. It certainly means that, in just over 40 years, the company has expanded dramatically from one single set of trade plates.

It was Roland Wilson who founded the Autocar Conveying Company about 1946, basing his business in an old stone quarry at Alvechurch. Wilson had been involved in an accident causing an injury to his leg which ruled out normal factory work. Austin Motors suggested that if he were to invest in a set of trade plates, they would put plenty of delivery business his way. Within five or six years, Wilson had expanded on this promise to have 45 sets of trade plates at work for him.

Though it might sound easy, the job of delivering a brand new vehicle didn't exactly live up to everything you might imagine. The driver had to be extremely considerate to his charge: to ensure their vehicles weren't abused on the run out to that distant retailer, Austin put a sticker in the rear window which read, 'If this vehicle exceeds 30 mph, please report the facts to the Austin Motor Co.' In 1952, very few new cars were fitted with even the most basic of heaters as standard, and those that were invariably had it fitted after the car had been delivered to the retailing dealer. And there was worse – driving a heaterless car from Birmingham to Kent in the heart of winter may have been marginally uncomfortable, but it was close to luxurious when compared to driving an open goods vehicle chassis at the same time of year. A wooden seat was all you had to sit on and all that protected the driver from the elements was a sheet of cardboard placed in front of his legs.

Norman Parker, now Managing Director at Autocar, joined the company in 1952 as a plater driver and he can still remember how icicles used to form on his flying suit as he virtually froze to the wheel. Unfortunately for the plater, who was only paid for whatever he delivered, the seasonal fluctuation in body-building costs between summer and winter meant that most of these open chassis were moved round the country during the winter period to take advantage of the cheaper rate.

One regular haul by the platers was to bring open chassis and trailer outfits from Scotland down to the Midlands for body construction. Norman recalls running with a group of about six similar vehicles on one occasion and stopping at the Jungle Cafe near Shap on the A6 to thaw out for a while. Last vehicle into the car park was driven by one of the platers known as 'Snuffer' because of his liking for that nostril-clearing powder. 'It won't pull the skin off a rice pudding,' Snuffer complained as the reason for being so far behind the

By 1962 Autocar had adopted their current name, a more suitable version than the original title of Autocar Conveying Company. This Austin tractive unit rated as a 17-tonner was the third generation of Austins used in six years, the original motive power having been bonneted Austin Loadstars fitted with the Perkins P6 engine. Little had changed in the Carrimore semi-trailer, for its brilliant swinging-link concept was to ensure that this load carrier was to last more than 15 years as an operators' first choice. With the Mini being particularly popular in the early 1960s, Autocar could regularly guarantee a six-car load even in the days when the maximun permitted overall length of an artic was a very short 35 feet.

others. 'It just wants the timing setting up,' said Sid Williams, another plater, who did all-in wrestling when he wasn't running up and down the road. 'I'll fix it for you.'

Sure enough, when the vehicles left the Jungle, Snuffer came from last to first in the convoy with a rare display of speed. It did however take the rest a further 20 miles to catch up and stop him to point out that the reason he was going so fast was that Sid Williams had disconnected the trailer and he had left it in the car park.

Plating was a precarious living. For regular daily runs to, say, London or Kent, you were issued with a season rail ticket for the return journey home. To make sure the boss got his money out of that rail ticket you worked that entire season flat out. In contrast, the roamers used to get expenses to cover the trip back but on arrival at the depot there was little guarantee of a job the next day. The plating game was rife with casual staff, shift workers like policemen, who would do a trip just for the pocket money on their day off. If that wasn't bad enough, the advent of the transporter designed for moving cars, at least, in vast numbers, brought a rapid decline in the amount of work available as the prospect of buying a new car with no mileage on the clock became too strong a selling point to be ignored.

About 1956, Autocar joined the early pioneers, investing in their first trio of specialist load carriers with Perkins P6-engined Austin Loadstar tractive units linked to the very popular Carrimore Mark 2 semi-trailers. Autocar were first contracted running solely export traffic for Austin Motors. Their four or five-car loads went wherever there were waiting deep-sea ships which could mean ports as far apart as London or Glasgow. Due to a strange interpretation of the relevant law at that time, Autocar's transporters were able to haul these export-bound cargos whilst displaying only the temporary type of general trade plate, which gave the holder far more choice of usage than the alternative limited type of trade plate. But as the transporter fleet expanded, the need for deliveries to home-market outlets meant the outfits had to be registered in the normal fashion.

Although car transporter operators at present tend to work directly for a car manufacturer or importing concessionaire, 30 years ago people like Autocar were employed by the individual garages or fleet outlets who had bought the newly made cars from the factory. One such agreement filled by Autocar was delivering Austins to the chain of Mumford's garages based in Plymouth. By 1962, Autocar had grown to run about 16 artic transporters and, sensing that the delivery business was in the ascendancy, Mumfords bought out the transporter company from Roly Wilson. To take over the management of Autocar, Mumfords – who operated under the title of Western Motor Holdings – brought in one Stan Alton. Some thought it a strange step, as he had no form of 'car' experience, but what

This Carrimore photograph illustrates what was to be the flagship of the Plymouth Transport Co. SJY 545 dates from 1960 and was in fact a 'Chinese Six' Leyland Steer with its second steering axle removed, this procedure being adopted to give a longer chassis length than the standard Leyland four-wheeler, the Beaver, could offer. Originally painted in Plymouth's colours, the vehicle was brought into the Autocar fleet when the Mumford family bought the transporter concern out. Remembered as being a good but rather slow outfit, the Leyland was run mainly between Birmingham and Plymouth before being switched onto the Midlands-Newcastle haul.

Accepted as having been the pioneers of moving individual cars on trade plates as a delivery business, B.J. Henry were to be bought out by Western Motor Holdings in the early 1960s and brought under the control of the Autocar organization. Henry had also been one of the first operators to use the double-deck car transporter and although they did run some of the favoured Carrimore-plus-Brockhouse outfits, 30 JFC is here coupled to a Taskers semi-trailer fitted with Burtonwood tail lift. Although having comparable lengths of carrying deck, the Taskers could be a tail-happy outfit because of the extra weight of the lift attached at the extreme rear.

he did bring was tremendous transport know-how and, under his control, the Autocar Group were to work themselves towards the top of the pack.

Like less specialized goods hauliers at that time, the car transporter men too were plagued with difficulties in winning extra carriers' licences from the transport authorities. If you bought out a smaller operator, you could get round this problem for not only did you acquire his vehicles and licences, you also bought both his goodwill and his list of customers. Mumfords chose this way of expanding, but although B.J. Henry, for example, was a highly thought-of acquisition, it was to be the name of Autocar which was retained as this and other operators were merged under Alton's control.

Along with a strange collection of lorries and an even stranger collection of trailers, Autocars were also to inherit a number of varied operating yards and depots which were required as intermediate storage posts for the new vehicles en route from the factory to the buying garage. A pair of such premises in close proximity on Bristol Road, Birmingham

had originally had two different owners prior to their selling out to the Western Group. All that separated the two was a large double-fronted house with an even larger rear garden stretching way back beyond the two yards. A slice of that garden to join the two depots would make all the difference in operating efficiency, but the owner had no intention of selling, no matter what the price. Norman Parker, tempted away from behind the steering wheel into the footholds of junior management, was given what seemed the impossible job of merging those two small Bristol Road yards. No amount of persuasion would prevail until Norman noticed that there was no garage to this house, the space on either side of the frontage being owned by Autocar. 'What if we traded a piece of land at the front so you can build a garage for a slice of the garden at the rear?' was his suggestion, immediately agreed upon.

With Autocar expanding quickly, the Alvechurch quarry soon became far too small and in 1967 they moved into their current 43-acre site at Wythall. Austin Motors had used the location as a storage area for some time prior to '67, and the

Dealers Deliveries, although having depots throughout the Midlands, were to base their operations at Luton and on Vauxhall/ Bedford movements. This Vauxhall photograph taken on March 27, 1961 was to celebrate the production of the 200,000th Bedford van. The CA was also produced in the open chassis form shown for the later fitment of specialized bodywork. To ensure three vehicles could be carried on the top deck of the Carrimore trailer, the first chassis was reversed on board. This required the outfit to be jacknifed prior to lowering the deck so that the projecting chassis didn't foul the back of the TK Bedford cab. The two saloon cars on the bottom deck are examples of the Vauxhall Victor (front) and Velox (rear).

By 1966 the fortunes of Autocar had changed dramatically. From about 16 transporters when taken over by Mumfords in 1962, the fleet quickly grew through other mergers and investment in vehicles, some idea of the expansion being given by this outfit's fleet number, 160. The original colour scheme of claret and beige, based on the Austin Motors livery, had gone in favour of a less austere green. The semi-trailer being hauled here was built by Harvey in Scotland. With its screw-thread lifted upper deck, the unit was supported on smaller tyres, giving the load a lower height for improved stability.

Dealers Deliveries were to be absorbed into the Dependable Delivery arm of the Autocar/Mumford organization. Although many transporter operators tended to follow a political influence when choosing tractor units – they normally selected the manufacturer who also made the cars they were carrying – Dealers were recalled as using all sorts of different motive units. There is not a great deal of weight for this Gardner-powered Foden to haul, but the load of historic cars from the National Motor Museum at Beaulieu, seen in the background, was probably one of the most valuable it would ever move. The semi-trailer is a Hoynor Mark 7, introduced about 1971 and still in current use nearly 20 years on.

Which method to use for exporting vehicles is always a decision that the car manufacturer has to make. Shipping them out in a fully completed form means that a high standard of finish can be guaranteed. However, this photograph was taken at Wythall in 1972 to show how much fresh air cars contain. The message of the shot is that in CKD form (completely knocked down) all the vehicles shown here – 50 Minis and Mini Clubmen – could be carried in the one container parked at the rear. Also on comparable show are the Hoynor Mark 2 semi-trailer on the left and the Carrimore Mark 9 on the right, which offered a similar capacity but in two different fashions. Autocar used many of these Albion Chieftain/Clydesdale tractor units around this time although the lack of interior headroom in the cab is recalled as one reason why their drivers didn't like them.

premises had earlier been an old RAF barrage-balloon station where winches, trailers and of course balloons had been worked on.

A similar expansion of operations was developed in the Cowley area of Oxford following the B.J. Henry acquisition, and Mumfords were then to turn their attention towards Luton and make massive inroads with Vauxhall/Bedford traffic. Motor Vehicle Collection (MVC) and Dealers Deliveries were two companies that were quickly absorbed, though not directly under the Autocar name, for all Luton-based vehicles were to be run in the title of another Western Group take-over, Dependable Deliveries.

Both Autocar and Dependable outfits were eventually painted in the same basic green and white colours, a livery that originated from The Plymouth Transport Co connection. Once the respective fleets were shaken down, standardization in tractors followed, until close to 90% of

the fleet was based on Leyland Group vehicles. The remainder were to be TK or KM Bedfords. Autocar had been famous for their allegiance to the long-serving, much favoured AEC Mandators, because the Leyland Buffalo's engine never stood the pace as well as the similar AEC power pack. Then, once Autocar started taking delivery of the TM Bedford tractors, they were to experience an entirely new type of operational problem.

The semi-trailers had to be kept as low as possible to cut down on damage caused by low trees to the top-deck cars, but the high, upright cab fitted to the TM Bedford was not immediately compatible with a semi-trailer once used behind a low-slung Mandator. With the top deck of the trailer extending far forward, above the cab of the tractor, Autocar found that in extreme articulation, the two would actually collide. It was difficult to believe, but drivers were reporting that if they were making a tight turn whilst

Winning the contract to move all Mann Egerton vehicles was an occasion recalled with pleasure by Autocar's Managing Director, Norman Parker. It also merited specially liveried vehicles, this AEC being seen brand new in 1975. Autocar were to run the Mandator tractive units until well into the 1980s, the low height of the cab giving ample space between its roof and the top deck of the trailer above it. The Carrimore Mark 9 semi-trailer in use here was recalled by some as being the finest car carrier to be built by Carrimore before being absorbed into the York trailer concern.

After early trials with the Leyland Roadtrain tractive unit, it has now become firmly established in the Autocar fleet. During 1985 the company invested more than £600,000 in 20 of these new units as part of an extensive replacement programme. Fitted with the Rolls-Royce 265Li engine and Spicer 10-speed gearbox, the Leyland is actually a day-cab unit fitted with a Jennings sleeper. This type of conversion was chosen as being more space-efficient, providing adequate cab accommodation yet still not intruding on the bottom-deck loading area.

Apart from that lone ex-Plymouth Transport Co Leyland Steer, Autocar had never run 'wagon and drag' outfits as standard in the past. The new technology developed together with Hoynor now means that at times the drawbar outfit can carry a regular load of eleven cars, compared to the artic's normal load of nine. Driver Mick Santer is seen with his Volve FL10-Hoynor outfit with a load of imported Peugeots and Citroens just loaded at Dover Docks. It's apparent from the crossover interlap of the loaded vehicles that the new breed of transporter demands a high degree of technological know-how from its operating staff.

negotiating a steep incline, when the trailer came back towards the straight ahead position it would hit the side of the tractor.

Representations to the truck manufacturers for a special low-profile cab solely for car transporter use didn't meet with any success so Autocar started to buy units like the Volvo F7 and DAF 2500 to combat this problem. Even the latest phase of Leyland Roadtrains and then Leyland-DAF 95 units have had to have their cabs specially lowered, and a very small sleeper cab fitted rather than the standard one, to save on valuable car carrying space.

All the current fleet – which also includes a 40% share of drawbar outfits, mainly on Volvo FL10 chassis – are painted in a cream-based livery under the single name of Autocar. The main priority affecting the operation of all the fleet is flexibility both in what they carry and how, but above all in where they carry from. Short-term contracts of perhaps only two years duration have to be applied for and, although a customer may well be pleased with good service, they do on occasion change over to a competitor because a cheaper price has been tendered. The current strategy sees about a third of the Autocar strength based at Richborough, near Dover, mainly involved in the movement of Citroen cars imported through Dover docks. Autocar do make use of the Cartic principle, shipping cars, especially to Scotland, by rail. But with the ability of the new 'wagon and drag' outfits

to carry 11 medium-size vehicles, road transport can be both more profitable and more efficient.

Running the long distance by rail does enable vast numbers of cars to be moved all at once but such a system can also see cars handled four different times whilst in transit. Autocar have five transporters currently based up at Bathgate to deliver the rail-hauled traffic. Road transporters too run north from Wythall, Ellesmere Port or any of their other depots into Bathgate so that these Scottish-based vehicles can also deliver their loads further north.

Autocar currently run on average about 68% of the time fully loaded, although the 17 transporters based at Coventry are able to run fully loaded all the time, backwards and forwards from Ryton to Dover with Peugeot vehicles in both directions. Running Ladas, once a Cartransport contract, has now been taken over by Autocar (the parent company bought out the interest of Lada UK) and as well as having 17 transporters based at Bridlington, the haulier also runs 11 curtainsider vehicles on Lada spares distribution. In 1987, financial control of Autocar effectively passed from the Western Group to Samuel Montagu & Co following its purchase of 54% of the shares. With 19 transporters based at Cowley and 19 based at Luton, the company still has 34 outfits based at Wythall, doing what they started out doing nearly 35 years ago, taking Austin exports to the docks. It's a fine record of service.

10: United Molasses Company

It must be the entrepreneur's dream. Find a product in great abundance unwanted by its producers, transport it to somewhere else, then, without doing anything to it, sell it on to a host of customers who are all clamouring to buy it. Although Michael Kroyer-Kielberg can't claim to have dreamt up the idea, it was his drive and vision that enabled the company of United Molasses and its subsidiaries to grow to the point of holding more than a 40% share of the world market. To some people Blackstrap Molasses, as it is known in the trade, was just a sheer embarrassment. All they wanted was a bottomless hole in the ground into which they could pour it. The thick, heavy, dark brown liquid is what remains after cane or beet has been refined to extract the maximum amount of sugar crystals. A chemist will tell you that this strong version of treacle, which still has a sweet smell and taste to it, is oozing with chemicals, minerals and vitamins which make it ideal in the production of animal feed. It is also required in the fermentation process. Whilst processing the UK's own, locally-grown sugar beet did mean that a certain amount of molasses was produced here, it could in no way meet the surge of demand created for both sugar and molasses at the start of the 20th century.

United Molasses as a company was officially launched on the stock exchange in January, 1926. It had been 19 years earlier than that, 1907, when Michael Kielberg, a 25-year-old Dane, came to Liverpool and took up a position with the importing concern of Marquis Clayton. Three years later, his expertise in the business had resulted in his becoming a partner to Clayton on the understanding that the molasses side of the business was his responsibility. And moving the stuff from place to place, of course, was a major part of the undertaking. In that brief period, Kielberg had identified that the established method of transporting molasses by ship in huge wooden barrels was totally inefficient.

In the following year, 1911, Clayton-Kielberg took the decision to erect the first of many storage tanks, on the other side of the country, in the port of Hull. The first shipment of 1,800 tons of molasses was discharged into the tank in early 1912 and the destiny of the company was laid. Tanks were then built on the Mersey at Garston and Birkenhead, and also at Greenock in Scotland. Whilst initially the molasses was transported on to its relevant customers in small wooden barrels, the forerunners of the famous United Molasses road tanker fleet weren't long in being ordered.

United was actually a coming together of two other companies, these being The British Molasses Co and The Pure Cane Molasses Co. Whilst United have long been established in the archives of transport history for the love and dedication they showed towards their Scammell road tankers, the two forerunners of United were actually plying their road tanker fleet long before Scammell Lorries had even been invented. To move those first shipments, they relied on a fleet of 15 lorries all made by the Glasgow company of Halley.

In their time, between 1901 and 1935, Halley were quite well known lorry builders, starting off with steam power before the transition to petrol. It was perhaps not a coincidence that United's first transport manager, R. Mackay-Walker, and the company's first vehicle engineer, George Wilson, had both started their transport service working at the Halley factory. It may well have been part of the original package in which so many new road tankers were purchased. As far as the drivers were concerned, the Halley was a huge, big, solid, dumb machine. All originally came as four-wheelers, and their size is best appreciated when you hear that they were converted into trailing-axle six-wheelers simply by slipping a third axle into the space left behind the original drive axle without having to modify anything else on the vehicle. It was George Wilson who carried out the conversions at the United garage in Ford Street, which reflects well on his expertise as a vehicle engineer.

It was in late 1912 that the partnership of Clayton and Kielberg received their first bulk shipment of blackstrap molasses, all 1,800 tons of it off-loaded into static tanks situated in Hull. In the following year, a receiving tank was erected at Garston in the southern suburbs of Liverpool. Although the molasses was originally shipped thence to customers in wooden barrels, an interim step taken prior to conventional road tankers arriving was to use demountable tanks drawn by traditional horse power. The combination pictured here belongs to Harpers, a respected name in Liverpool around that time, whose large stabling provided a lot of horse-drawn transport. The contented look on the horse's face may be because molasses was used a great deal in the production of horse feed made by The Molassine Company, absorbed into the United Molasses Company in 1971.

One idiosyncrasy of the Halley was that the huge gearshift lever was mounted to the right of the driver rather than being centrally mounted for the driver's left hand. This positioning in turn meant a complicated gearshift linkage which sadly wasn't averse to seizure. Driver Elijah Grant, who drove fleet number 14, grew sick of this continual sticking between gears so, to solve the problem, he carried with him a walking stick which was sharpened at one end. When the change mechanism stuck, Elijah had off to a fine art the technique of pushing the walking stick through the floor to move the linkage round and select the correct cog.

Robert Mackay-Walker – known only to his closest friends as Bob – may well have been a strong Halley man, but he wasn't short-sighted about their failings. So when Scammell announced the brilliant concept of articulated eight-wheeled tankers in 1922, Mackay-Walker quickly sensed their potential and four brand new ones were soon to join the fleet of Pure Cane.

One of the big problems with molasses is that it is so relatively heavy. With a specific gravity of 1.4, it is twice the weight of, say, the same number of gallons of petrol. To counteract this, the big attraction of these new Scammells was that they were so light. The concept of having a frameless semi-trailer – no chassis but just the tank bridging the gap between the tractor unit and the trailer bogie wheels – was years ahead of its time.

With the arrival of this first quartet of Watford's finest, United were to attach their allegiance to the Scammell flag, a partnership to which they remained faithful for over 50 years. Whilst the followers of this fleet would tend to remember the resplendent Routeman eight-wheelers, the men who worked and drove for United would probably want to tell you about the feats of a far less obviously charismatic Scammell.

When the bulk molasses carriers became mechanized, it was the Glasgow lorry builder Halley who was to provide the first 15 or so tankers. KC 7175 dates from 1922 and originally it came to Liverpool as a four-wheeler shod with solid tyres. Fleet engineer George Wilson carried out the trailing-axle conversion of this tanker without having to stretch the original chassis. Along with the change to pneumatics, UM also fitted electrics for the lighting to augment the original carbide lamps. The Halley was remembered as a particularly heavy and unresponsive machine but it was kept in use until about 1938. Jim Pope was regular driver of fleet number 15 which had its petrol engine fed from a roof-mounted fuel tank.

Once Scammell announced their new articulated eight-wheelers (four wheels in line on the trailer axle), it wasn't long before they were bought by UM as bulk carriers. The idea of a frameless tanker – brilliant in its conception – made the vehicle that much lighter, and ideal for heavy blackstrap molasses. George Baker identifies YX 5470 as chassis number 1246, fitted with a four-cylinder petrol engine. Pure Cane Molasses Co was a concern formed in 1921; for all practical terms this name was to be dropped in 1926 when the United Molasses Company was floated on the stock exchange as a holding company for the interests of both Pure Cane and The British Molasses Co.

In total, United were to buy about 12 Mechanical Horses. Announced originally at the 1933 London Commercial Motor Show, there were two basic versions of either 3 or 6-ton capacity. However, the sheer density of molasses meant that when the Horse's semi-trailer tankers were filled, they were running close to 10 tons. Pottering round the animal feed mills of Merseyside with a top speed capability of around 16mph, this extra bit of weight wasn't much of a problem but once they went into the Mersey Tunnel it became quite a headache. For obvious reasons, a minimum speed limit of 6mph was imposed on all vehicles. Although going down into the bottom of the tunnel was a case of hanging on and not letting the Horse run away, climbing out the other side was foot to the boards and stay flat out in bottom gear. 6½mph was what the drivers reckoned they were doing, well above that 6mph limit, but it still didn't stop the rumbles of discontent from those following.

The United driving staff were totally faithful both to their vehicles and their company, for United Molasses as an employer with Kielberg as the Managing Director was something special. Whilst keeping in employment of any kind was difficult in the recession-hit late 1920s and early 1930s, United was a go-ahead firm that rewarded loyal service. Pension schemes, long before anyone else even thought about them, plus hefty bonuses were among the incentives that kept men like Tom Williams and Norman Byrne at UM from boyhood garage apprenticeships right up to retirement – wartime service excepted. Williams was to follow Mackay-Walker up to the post of Transport Manager, Byrne to the post of Fleet Engineer, but both started their UM careers in a much more basic way.

It may not be done now, but in the early 1930s it was the apprentices' first job at 6.30 on a morning to start the tanker engines up on the handle and let them tick over for 15 or 20 minutes to warm up that thick engine oil. Starting any lorry on the handle was an art in itself but for a 14-year-old 'can lad' – the boy whose main job was to make cans of tea – it was

a major achievement, with the erratic timing on the Halley's petrol engine causing unpredictable kick-back.

It was a major turning point when electric starters first appeared on the new lightweight Scammell artic units and then with their famous Rigid 8. Scammell weren't the first to produce a rigid eight-wheeler, in fact they were probably one of the last, but what saw the light of day in 1937 was to have a production run of over 20 years. Designed by Oliver North and engineered under the direction of Percy Hugh, the Gardner 6LW-powered Scammell R8 was immediately in huge demand. United Molasses, like many, were to appreciate the vehicle's lightness, and the engineering of the famous six-speed constant-mesh gearbox and the revolutionary epicyclic drive axle made for very few service problems in those areas of the vehicle.

One area which did create difficulty was in getting traction on the single-drive rear bogie, especially when climbing empty over ice and snow covered Pennine roads during the winter time. Tom Williams was to play a major role in the development of a chain-drive kit which could link the axles and thus drive the trailing axle of the rear bogie from the driven one. Its concept was similar to the gear-driven rear bogie of the Scammell Pioneer. But the United drivers felt they were awkward to fit and tended to run without them, relying on their driving skill to get them through.

The United Scammell R8 driver of the 1940s and '50s was generally speaking a Liverpudlian. Although UM were to expand their storage facilities round the ports of the UK to take in places like Bristol, Dagenham and Belfast as well as the established Liverpool, Hull and Greenock facilities, the road tanker fleet was always based at 10, Blenheim Street, Liverpool, and controlled from there even though the company's administrative head offices were in London. The one big exception to this rule was during what was called 'The Campaign'. To cater for the surge in molasses production during the UK sugar beet season of October to

Opposite, above: this postwar photograph shows the two types of Scammell at opposite ends of the scale which were to perform outstanding work for United Molasses. Seen loading at the Birkenhead terminal from overhead facilities, BKA 128, which dates from 1935, was an example of what was called the lightweight Scammell tractor unit. Still powered by petrol, its engine had two aluminium cylinder heads with phosphor bronze inserts for the valves. Norman Byrne recalls that this vehicle ran with the petrol engine until about 1946 when a Gardner 6LW diesel was fitted. It was then sold to Ireland where it ran for more than 15 years hauling the same type of molasses traffic for the Irish Sugar Co. GKB 755, one of the many Mechanical Horses run by UM, dates from 1942. Opposite, below: once the Scammell Mechanical Horses had been put out to grass, UM tried a variety of tractive units to haul the smaller loads. This Seddon dating from 1953 hauled one of the older Scammell single-axle semi-trailers that had been operated with the Horses. Powered by the P6 Perkins engine, the Seddon was capable of reaching 40mph, which was twice the speed limit applicable in the early 1950s. UM engineers fitted an extra vacuum cylinder to try and boost the stopping power of the brakes. Quite often, however, it was simply a case of the driver relying on sheer brute strength. Above: the Scammell Rigid 8, along with the later Routeman, was to be the flagship of United Molasses throughout the period of postwar expansion and up until the 1970s. First conceived in 1936, it went into production in 1937 and was still being produced 20 years later. UKD 396 dates from 1956 and by that time the R8 was starting to look rather old-fashioned with its split windscreen which could be opened. (It's interesting to note that the first batch of Scammell R8s made in '37 did not have this type of double split screen.) Many changes had gone on underneath the Scammell's skin in its 20 years. The option of super single tyres on the rear bogie was a Watford trademark that is only recently coming back into vogue on the modern eight-legger. Below: there were to be somewhat less than 100 Routeman Mark 1s built and it was fitting that United Molasses were to take delivery of both the first one and the last one. Two examples, 106 and 111, are seen at the Regent Road storage depot in Liverpool. 106 was the second Routeman following consecutively after 105 DKF (Tom Williams, the UM transport manager, had long ago created a system where the fleet number of a vehicle coincided with its registration). Fitted with the Gardner 6LX engine, these eight-wheelers were run by UM for 14 years continuous, faithful operation. The first Leyland influence on the Scammell eight was that the Routeman had the frame and steering axles also fitted to the Leyland Octopus.

February, about ten tankers would be based between Kings Lynn, Ely, Colchester and London, ferrying the beet molasses – a less viscous liquid and easier to handle – round the plants of eastern England. This spell of living in digs for up to six weeks made a change in the driver's working pattern, although there had always been the case when individual vehicles had been requested to work out of those distantly located storage plants. Generally it was a small Mechanical Horse that was sent out from Liverpool to work out of Hull or even Bristol, where trudging the leafy lanes of South Devon was how those trusty steeds gave faithful service. When they did eventually go, the Horses were replaced by a mixture of Bedford and Seddon tractor units, the original Scammell trailers and couplings being transferred to the new generation of tractive unit.

The new generation of Scammell eight-wheelers came in November 1959, and it was perhaps rather fitting that United Molasses were to receive the first Routeman to be built, registration number 105 DKF. This tanker had the fleet number 105, Tom Williams having long ago devised a system by which the registration mark of the vehicle somehow coincided with the fleet number. UM were also to buy the last of the Routeman 1s to be made: in total, there were less than 100 of these eight-wheelers produced, of which about 30 came to Liverpool's United.

In April 1965, ownership of United Molasses passed into the hands of Tate & Lyle but it wasn't until the 1970s that the whole structure and working pattern of the tanker fleet was to change, under the influence of Rocky Prior. Up to the time of his arrival, United's Scammells tended to have a 14-year life of service with the company. It was a long time, especially for a goods vehicle, and although the yearly mileage was never excessive, just keeping a vehicle of that age running every day meant high workshop costings. At a stroke, Prior introduced a maximum of eight years as a vehicle's life, and six new Scammell Crusaders were promptly ordered as replacements for some of the ageing Routemen. United could certainly have the new tractors – provided they could wait 18 months, so in sheer frustration they turned to the growing band of importers to fill this urgent need.

Magirus-Deutz had set up just down the road at Winsford, and in contrast they asked for just a fortnight to deliver as many rigid eight-wheelers and 4x2 tractive units as United wished to take. Rocky had already had some good experience of the Maggie air-cooled engines, so up to about a half of the United fleet of 60 to 70 vehicles was eventually Magirus based. They proved very reliable in service,

Driver Joe Illingworth, a great Scammell man, is pictured at Crossfield Mill discharging from fleet number 125, a Routeman Mark 1 of 1961 vintage. The wooden horse-trough type receiving funnel, which looks rather antiquated, was actually a very efficient way of discharging a cargo of molasses. At a fairly warm temperature it would only take 15 to 20 minutes to unload by this method which was of course only possible if the receiving mill had underground storage facilities. The vast majority of drop-off points had high-mounted storage tanks and this could mean that anything up to 4 hours was spent in blowing off a full load of molasses.

Although Thompsons of Bilston and occasionally Andrews of Liverpool had been the main tank manufacturers used by United Molasses, the company went to Crane Fruehauf to produce a number of three-compartment semi-trailers which went into service in November 1982. UM, like many other concerns, were anticipating the raising of maximum permitted artic weights from 32 tons to 38 tonnes. To ensure their vehicles never exceeded the lower applicable weight, the outfits were originally run on four axles and with the smaller centre compartment empty. After the law changed in May 1983, the tank builder slipped a third axle under the semi-trailer so allowing UM to use the third compartment and quickly make the operational jump to 38 tonnes. The change to Foden tractor units is also reflected in this scene.

although with the general trend towards larger capacity engines, they did seem a little down on power. The vehicles were also rather expensive on parts so, for the next phase of tankers, UM were to think long and hard about which direction to follow. The promotion of Ken Simmons to London in 1976 as UK Transport Manager saw the arrival of two new units intended for long term appraisal.

Simmons had started with United Molasses at their Bristol depot and in using subcontractor's vehicles for occasional molasses movements had been fairly impressed with the ERF tankers run by Stamps. Leonard Stamp spoke very highly of the Cummins-powered ERF with a Fuller gearbox and Rockwell drive axle, these observations being borne out by experience with the two vehicles put into service by United. Another 16 ERFs were to follow around 1979. But it was to be a performance in Africa that eventually convinced United's management to opt for another British-made truck, albeit with the same form of drivetrain as their current ERFs.

In search of copious quantities of molasses, the United men of old had travelled far and wide. The growth of sugar cane is limited to an area 30 degrees north or south of the equator which is also served with an adequate supply of rainfall. Although Cuba and the West Indies were the first sources of sugar and molasses, this market went sour, forcing Michael Kielberg eventually to choose Java in the Dutch East Indies as his main source in 1924. A round trip by sea to Java in those days took 2½ months so it was obvious that ships, the larger the better, were to become a major part of the United Molasses organization to meet their own growing demands. The 'Theodore F. Reynolds', later to be renamed 'Athelstane' was the company's first small bulk carrier, bought second-hand in 1922, but in less than 15 years, what was to be named The Athel Shipping Line was to have a fleet of more than 20 larger vessels and was destined to grow even more.

The problems of shipping molasses from all parts of the globe were quickly sorted by United, but in Sudan at the beginning of the 1980s the company was faced with the problem of hauling their favoured product some 800 miles from the various inland sugar factories to Port Sudan for onward shipment. The railway system was unable to cope with the increasing volume of molasses being moved so UM decided that greater dependence would have to be placed on

While this vehicle's area of operation is given away by its registration number, United Molasses followers will also recognize the significant style of the letter M in the company name as an indication that this molasses carrier works out of UM's Belfast depot. The Leyland-badged Constructor 8 rigid built at the Scammell factory has now re-established a strong niche for itself back in the United Molasses fleet after losing out in favour of first Magirus and then Foden rigids. Pictured in December 1986, the L10-250 Cummins-powered Leyland fitted with the nine-speed Fuller range-change gearbox is in fact carrying the tanker body that was originally fitted to a UM Maggie eight-legger, fleet number 237. The pipes running down the side of the tank are drain hoses that are used should there be a spillage or overflow occurring in the top box of the barrel.

a road transport operation. The company had discussions with various expatriate hauliers working in the Sudan, including Wynns Heavy Haulage, about back-loading molasses but in the end it was Amalgamated Transport who were able to undertake the work, using United's own demountable 20-tonne capacity tank containers. At that time, Amalgamated had a fleet of Fodens and Volvos but it was the Cummins-powered vehicles from the UK that appeared to be best able to stand up to the testing work. Four containers at a time on a double-bottom outfit meant 80 tonnes of molasses was hauled out on every journey.

Although the UK laws would never allow such generous payloads as in the Sudan, the performance that was demonstrated there helped United to select competitively priced Cummins-powered Foden tractor units to take the company into the 38-tonne weight band. This took place at the start of 1983, the outfits being worked in a 2+3 configuration, whilst the Foden eight-wheeler was also taken into the fleet to replace the similar rigid Maggies that were approaching their retiring age.

One area where the Foden eight-wheelers were to be questioned was when they were used in rural conditions. Although large compounders and other industrial outlets were United tankers' main destinations, there was a growing market for molasses, now available in blended varieties, direct to farmers in bulk for their own animal feed production. The Foden eight-wheeler seemed rather awkward in these situations and when tests were made by UM they found that the Watford-built Leyland Constructor 8s were slightly more manoeuvrable, having a smaller turning circle than the similar Foden. Fitting these new Leyland-badged vehicles with lightweight aluminium tanks also produced close to 20 tonnes of payload capacity, almost a tonne more than the steel Foden tanker.

In a way, it was similar to the discovery made by R. Mackay-Walker way back in 1922 that led to the introduction of the new vogue of lightweight Scammells into the United fleet. These latest Constructors were amongst the last vehicles to be built at Watford before the Scammell factory was closed and production transferred to Leyland in Lancashire.

For maximum weight/payload operation, capable of hauling 26.3 tonnes of molasses, United have now selected as their current fleet flagship the latest E-series Cummins-powered ERF tractor unit, a marque of vehicle that firmly established our second own-account operator.

Fleet List
UNITED MOLASSES COMPANY

Fleet no	Reg no	Make	Model	Registered
250	BKA 620X	Foden	O8RO30C2410	1/10/81
251	BKA 621X	Foden	O8RO30C2410	8/10/81
252	BKA 622X	Foden	O8RO30C2410	16/10/81
253	BKA 623X	Foden	O8RO30C2410	26/10/81
254	BKA 624X	Foden	O8RO30C2410	2/11/81
255	BKA 625X	Foden	O8RO30C2410	10/11/81
256	BKA 626X	Foden	O8RO30C2410	17/11/81
257	BKA 627X	Foden	O8RO30C2410	25/11/81
258	BKA 628X	Foden	O8RO30C2410	2/12/81
260	EEM 22Y	Foden	S104	1/11/82
261	EEM 23Y	Foden	S104	4/11/82
262	EEM 24Y	Foden	S104	4/11/82
263	EEM 25Y	Foden	S104	4/11/82
264	EEM 26Y	Foden	S104	4/11/82
265	EEM 27Y	Foden	S104	16/11/82
266	EEM 28Y	Foden	S104	23/11/82
267	A770 HTJ	Leyland-Scammell	A8T57P3000C25	19/12/82
268	A771 HTJ	Leyland-Scammell	A8T57P3000C25	1/01/84
269	A772 HTJ	Leyland-Scammell	A8T57P3000C25	1/02/84
270	A773 HTJ	Foden	S104	1/03/84
271	A774 HTJ	Foden	S104	1/05/84
272	A775 HTJ	Foden	S104	7/02/84
273	B852 LKD	Foden	S104	1/10/84
274	B853 LKD	Foden	S104	1/10/84
275	B854 LKD	Foden	S104	1/10/84
276	B855 LKD	Foden	S104	1/10/84
277	B856 LKD	Foden	S104	1/10/84
278	B784 LKF	Leyland-Scammell	A8T57P3000C25LG	3/10/84
279	B785 LKF	Leyland-Scammell	A8T57P3000C25LG	3/10/84
280	C651 OKF	Foden	S104	1/10/85
281	C652 OKF	Foden	S104	1/10/85
282	C653 OKF	ERF	297140C2TR5C1	1/11/85
283	C654 OKF	ERF	297140C2TR5C1	1/11/85
284	C655 OKF	ERF	297140C2TR5C1	1/11/85
285	C656 OKF	Leyland-Scammell	AT57P3000C25A	8/10/85
286	C657 OKF	Leyland-Scammell	AT57P3000C25A	1/10/85
287	D329 SKF	Foden	S104	3/10/86
288	D330 SKF	Foden	S104	3/10/86
289	D331 SKF	Foden	S104	29/10/86
290	D332 SKF	ERF	315438C2TRSR1	9/10/86
291	D333 SKF	ERF	315438C2TRSR1	4/11/86
292	D334 SKF	ERF	315438C2RTSR1	1/12/86
293	D335 SKF	ERF	315438C2RTSR1	1/12/86
294	E802 WKF	ERF	354U40C2TRSR1	1/03/88
295	E803 WKF	ERF	354U40C2TRSR1	1/03/88
296	E689 WKC	Leyland-Scammell	A8T57P3000C25LG	8/02/88
297	E690 WKC	Leyland-Scammell	A8T57P3000C25LG	8/02/88
298	E691 WKC	Leyland-Scammell	A8T57P3000C25LG	8/02/88

11: SVW Distribution Ltd

To some manufacturers who produce their own goods, getting them delivered to their respective customers is just a necessary evil. Not for them is the involvement in buying lorries, employing drivers and organizing deliveries; it is far easier just to pick up the telephone and ring up their friendly local haulier. Doing it this way means the product is normally hidden beneath anonymous sheets or curtains with only the name of the haulier on show (though it is a growing habit to have a dedicated contract vehicle done out in a customer's agreed livery). Generally speaking, it is the haulier who reaps the harvest of all the free advertising made available by travelling the millions of road miles that haulage vehicles annually acrue.

One notable exception to the general rule is a company who can well vouch for the power of advertising. Were it not for the combination of a distinctive motif, a name which immediately stuck in the minds of the general public and a well targeted campaign on commercial television, then the most well known invention of one Francis Showering – the drink 'Babycham' – might never have stood the test of time.

Though it's nearly 40 years since the most famous drink produced in Shepton Mallet came to the fore, the Showerings can trace their connections with that north Somerset town back to the 17th century. The family's trade had been first in shoemaking, and then hotel keeping before turning to brewing and cider making. It was in 1843 that Francis Showering bought the fire-burnt remnants of the Ship Inn in Kilver Street together with some surrounding land. His ideas were progressively developed and his four grandsons, Herbert, Arthur, Ralph and Francis formed the limited company of Showerings Ltd in 1932.

It is a matter of public record that the invention of Babycham, officially accredited to Francis, was to create a business explosion which surprised many by its sheer intensity – none more so perhaps than Simon Neale. Originally joining the company in 1937 to work in the accounts department, by the early 1950s he had moved on to become a travelling salesman, based at lodgings in Hayes, Middlesex. The fortunes of Showerings then depended on people like Simon banging on doors and trying to interest one and all in the brews of north Somerset. With the power of commercial television being far greater than the single smooth-talking voice, Simon's technique was made redundant as ITV developed, and he was hauled back to Somerset to face more pressing problems. For the remaining 23 years of his working life at Showerings he, like many others, was to be taxed with the problems of distributing the newly invented drink that everyone was crazy about.

The demand made for the Christmas rush in 1954 totally overwhelmed the supply from the Shepton Mallet site and for nearly two years Showerings had to operate a quota system whilst production was slowly increased in such a way that the very high quality of the drink was retained. Had Babycham been conceived today, Showerings would simply have consulted some of the big names in contract distribution and asked them to suggest a delivery package. In the early 1950s no such concept of contract work existed, for whilst British Road Services virtually monopolized long-distance general haulage, they weren't geared up to meet the exacting needs of the Showering brothers. There was really no alternative; the manufacturers had to get on and deliver the product themselves.

Selecting the tool of the trade was done on a 'try it and see' basis but ERFs quickly impressed and the arrival of the futuristic KV cab from the Sandbach producer finally swung the decision ERF's way. All configurations of ERF were eventually to run in the Showering colour scheme of two-tone blue, but the backbone – close to 70% – of the long-distance fleet were all four-wheeled rigids.

A single product, one small bottle, with a single serving of that sparkling perry drink, was delivered nationwide on the backs of those distinctive Showerings ERFs. The convoys leaving Shepton Mallet were a classic sight in the late 1950s as they headed north on a Sunday afternoon. A chain of four distributing depots were set up in London, Manchester, Glasgow and Aberdeen but it could mean a round trip of 1,200 miles to that Granite City carrying full bottles north and of course bringing a full load of empty bottles back. It is perhaps no surprise that some of these little four-wheelers would clock up half-a-million miles in a chassis that was only six years old.

At the heart of their vehicles, Showerings were totally committed to the Gardner engine. Mainly the four-cylinder plodders, but with heavier weights then obviously the bigger five and six-pot versions were used, right up to the top-of-the-range Gardner 6LX-150. For the next 20 years Showerings remained faithful to the ERF/Gardner combination to deliver their products, although with a series of mergers and take-overs, the types of drinks being carried were set to diversify dramatically. In 1956, Showerings were to buy the company of Redvers Coate, who had been in cider production since 1925 at Nailsea near Bristol. Five years on,

they bought the cyder producers Gaymers, the differing spelling of the drink being one indication that the product from Attleborough, Norfolk, is of an entirely different taste to the produce of Somerset. In 1959, the Showering brothers had floated their booming business on the Stock Exchange and gone public. Two years later, Showerings were to tie up with Vine Products and Whiteways, the abbreviated title of SVW Distribution Ltd being the name adopted on the headboard of the delivery vehicles.

With SVW themselves being taken over by Allied Breweries, the Showering family were gradually to relinquish control, although their small-bottled creation continued its surge in popularity. Its peak year in production was about 1976, coinciding with a number of happenings in the transport world which were to have a major effect on the long-term development of SVW Distribution. The first major change was prompted by ERF's decision not to continue to fit the smaller Gardner engine in the four-wheeled rigid vehicle, still the mainstay of the SVW fleet. No amount of pleading would change ERF's mind so, as SVW weren't too happy with the alternative, they took the

Showerings Ltd were to acquire the company of William Gaymer & Sons Ltd in 1961. This photograph taken about 1930 illustrates the differing modes of distribution vehicle then in use. The quartet of Leylands are of a design similar to those made in hundreds for use by the Air Force during World War 1. Gaymers didn't need a very large road fleet as they tended to rely on the railway to distribute most of their products: in 1896 they had moved the five miles from Banham to Attleborough specifically so they could get onto the rail network. Although the photograph was taken at Attleborough, the drays and at least two of the Leylands were operated out of a sub-depot in Hackney Road, east London. The building in the background was the main bottling area which was hit by a stray German bomb in 1943 and extensively damaged.

Redvers Coate was a graduate of Bristol University who set up in cider production in 1925 at Nailsea near Bristol. Showerings took this concern over in 1956, but R.N. Coate continued to manufacture and deliver nationally from Nailsea until 1974 when production was transferred to a newly built plant at Shepton Mallett. Their delivery fleet peaked at a total of 34 during the mid-1960s, a mixed variety featuring Bedford KLMs, TKs and ERF 54G platforms. They also ran these two Albion Claymores which date from 1960. Although it was never built by Albion in large numbers, the Claymore, first made in 1954, was an ideal distribution vehicle as its engine was mounted in a flat, underfloor position.

Although Showerings were to run six and eight-wheeled rigids as well as ERF tractor units, it was the four-wheeled platform that was to be their famous trademark as it trunked Babycham to all parts of the UK mainland. The first ERFs bought in the mid-1950s were initially used on fruit collection from the Showering farms in Somerset and one of the farms is the backdrop for this four-wheeler which dates from 1962. The first four-wheelers had the Gardner 4LK engine and David Brown gearbox but into the 1960s, with the arrival of the first motorways, Showerings were to specify the more powerful five-pot Gardner 5LW engine for their well liked ERFs.

opportunity to look around the market-place and eventually settled on the Seddon Atkinson range. Oddly, the new 200 range wasn't Gardner powered either and even now the latest 211s have the Perkins Phaser engines fitted, but SVW did find the new range of vehicles entirely to their liking.

Babycham was being delivered abroad with two dedicated vehicles driven by Vic and Cyril Blinman who were doing weekly trips to Belgium commencing in 1976. Horrific reliability problems with the mandatory mechanical tachograph made SVW realize that once they became obliged to fit them for their UK vehicles, an awful amount of time would be spent in repairs, recalibrations or reseals. With the nearest tachograph fitting station being 25 miles away in Bristol, SVW eventually set up their own fitting station at Shepton Mallet, primarily to service their own vehicles but also greatly appreciated by other local truck and bus operators.

To meet the requirements of the tachograph manufacturers, SVW had to form a new company in the guise of Tachograph Services (Shepton Mallet) Ltd. In

It was in 1961 that Showerings were to merge with Vine Products and Whiteways, this resulting in the name SVW being coined for the distributing arm of the company. Vine Products are famous for their VP wines and QC sherries, the company having been founded by Alexander Mitzotakis in 1905. Their produce is made from imported concentrated grape juice which normally comes into the country to static storage tanks at Shoreham. Then, transported by road tanker, it is destined for the plants at Kingston-upon-Thames and Magdale near Huddersfield. Seen at the Marston Magna winery, LYC 486E was one of four road tanker outfits used on this dedicated wine traffic. Although it was permissible to run at 32 tons on four-axled artics after 1966, a strange requirement for outer axle spread meant, for a short while at least, in all practical terms 'Chinese Six' tractors like this Foden were needed to haul legally at this heavier weight band.

Although Babycham is now known throughout the world, the circular door logo on OYD 995F in this photograph ('Das Fruhlichste Getrank Der Welt') recalls an early export initiative undertaken by SVW in 1967 when this small 7-tonner went to Austria on delivery work. The bodywork made by Taylor Bros of Keynsham features Robinson door shutters. SVW had about 12 Commers in the fleet around the 1967 period, remembered as having particularly effective air brakes when compared to the similar-weight Bedfords. The company used this type of 11-ton gvw vehicle as well as the 12-ton gvw Commer, the latter having the Perkins 364 engine.

VYB 827M was the only foreign-made goods vehicle that Showerings were to buy. The Volvo was bought as a demonstrator with a view to comparing costings against similar ERF and Foden 32-ton tractor units. Although it stayed on fleet for seven years, the Volvo range-change gearbox is recalled as taking some getting used to. 'Nobby' Clarke is pictured at the wheel of the F88 whilst taking part in the Lorry Driver of the Year competition. Showerings encourage entry into this annual event and have partaken for over 20 years. Although the company has never had a national champion, it has had several national class winners, the most recent being drivers D. Rowsell and R. Hale.

Although it can have one or two drawbacks, curtainsider bodywork now features strongly on many SVW vehicles, from the smallest rigids up to the varying types of artic that the company uses. This 200-series Seddon Atkinson dates from 1978 and is actually a conversion from a 16-ton four-wheeled rigid. Used in articulated form FYA 293T was plated for 22 tons operation. This allowed for a clear 12-ton load on 12 pallets to be delivered. While the same weight of payload could be carried on a rigid six-wheeler, the extra load space, manoeuvrability and operational flexibility of a three-axled artic was to be of operational benefit to Showerings.

Opposite: as the name Tachograph Services (Shepton Mallet) Ltd suggests, this offshoot of Showerings was originally created to surmount the large hurdle of tachograph fitment instigated at the end of the 1970s. However, such was the expertise that developed, this company under the guidance of chief transport engineer Rodney Neale was able to undertake their own drop-frame conversions, starting from a standard four-wheeled cab and chassis. D398 LYB is one of these TS conversions which has a deck height of only 22 inches, with obvious advantages for local delivery work, and took to the road in October 1986. The distinctive livery gives maximum advertizing exposure to the brand leader Olde English Cyder, the different spelling of cider underlining the difference between the Somerset and East Anglia drinks.

In the 1970s Showerings made the transition from ERF to Seddon Atkinson as the standard marque for their four-wheeled distribution workhorse. For long-distance trunking work ERF artices still continued to be used but FYD 572T was one of three Foden 4x2 artic tractor units bought in 1978. This was done to carry out operational comparisons with the ERF although the 6LXC-powered Foden failed to impress the Shepton Mallet operator. The tandem-axle semi-trailer features Taylor Bros bodywork on Taskers running gear.

Once the Shepton Mallet operator had proved the worth of the 211 drop-frame, Seddon Atkinson adopted the idea to produce a similar vehicle at half the cost of TS's own in-house conversion. It was Walter Booth, the late chief engineer at Sed Atky, who took the concept over and improved slightly on it. Their modifications included lowering the vehicle's Perkins Phaser engine by two inches at the rear. E656 XYC is one of these Oldham-built vehicles, with regular driver Robin Maidment illustrating the ease of access at the lower height into the Taylor Bros body. The vehicle and driver are normally employed on long-distance multiple delivery work: the schedule normally means a payload of 8 tons is dropped off in 16 different deliveries on a round trip of about 360 miles.

typical Showerings style, the new fledgling company didn't simply rely on tachographs for work, for in no time they were fitting things like sideguards and spray suppression equipment, eventually developing to become a Seddon Atkinson agent.

The evolution of Tachograph Services was to bring a large element of self-sufficiency to the SVW fleet, which now tends to run in two basic colour schemes, the traditional but updated blue of Babycham and the brighter yellow of Gaymer's cyder. Seddon Atkinsons now totally dominate the list, with just a sprinkling of ERFs. But even the large number of 211s are starting to change in design following developments prompted by chief transport engineer Rodney Neale.

As quite a lot of their cargo had to be unloaded by hand, the staff soon let it be known that having a vehicle a lot closer to the ground can be of major benefit. To get the drop-frame vehicle they desired, Tachograph Services did the first conversions themselves. Using a municipal chassis type spring with a softer top leaf meant the hump over the drive axle was kept to a minimum. An Eaton narrow-track drive axle was also co-opted into the plan, allowing slider-door bodywork to be used for the entire length of the low-slung vehicle which was also fitted with Norde rubber suspension.

An extra benefit was that these succesful adaptions allowed an additional two pallets to be carried, so the concept was quickly taken on board by Seddon Atkinson who began to do this type of conversion before the rigids left the factory, which meant a price saving over the in-house job.

Another feature of the modern day SVW vehicles is that many are fitted with sleeper cabs, a reflection of the fact that these four-wheelers still do a great deal of mileage on their distributing hops. Currently in charge of distribution is Kevin O'Brien who has the use of three main centres that his goods emanate from, Shepton Mallet in the south west, Attleborough in the east and a purpose-built depot at Huddersfield in the north.

Tight co-ordination is the byword in today's traffic office and although the classic convoys of yesterday may not be too regular a sight today, SVW still move a phenomenal amount of drink, many tons of which are run inter-depot during the night. Following the tie-up with so many different well known brands, the SVW distribution manager now has the daunting prospect of a possible 700 different lines that his vehicles may deliver. These cover everything from fruit juices to Teacher's Whisky and Harvey's Bristol sherries as well as many millions of small bottles of a drink that only one man had the foresight to see a big future in.

Fleet List
SVW DISTRIBUTION LTD

Vehicles based at Shepton Mallet

No	Reg no	Make/model Type,GVW*		
95260	RFB 602S	ERF 4x2	T	
95262	YYB 598X	Leyland Freighter	R	16
95269	A79 NYD	ERF 6x2	T	
95272	A81 NYD	Sed Atk 6x2	T	
95274	A85 NYD	ERF 6x2	T	
95278	B138 VYD	Sed Atk 6x2	T	
95279	B137 VYD	Sed Atk 6x2	T	
95280	B136 VYD	Sed Atk 6x2	T	
95287	B144 VYD	Sed Atk 4x2	T	
95288	C194 DYA	Sed Atk 210	R	16
95289	C195 DYA	Sed Atk 4x2	T	
95290	D397 LYB	Sed Atk 210	R	16
95295	C201 DYA	Sed Atk 4x2	T	
95296	C202 DYA	Sed Atk 4x2	T	
95298	D399 LYB	Sed Atk 211	R	16
95299	D402 LYB	Sed Atk 6x2	T	
95300	D403 LYB	Sed Atk 6x2	T	
95301	D404 LYB	Sed Atk 6x2	T	
95302	D405 LYB	Sed Atk 6x2	T	
95303	D406 LYB	Sed Atk 6x2	T	
95304	E655 XYC	Sed Atk 211	R	16
95305	E562 TYA	Sed Atk 211	R	16
95306	E563 TYA	Sed Atk 211	R	16
95307	E564 TYA	Sed Atk 211	R	16
95308	E565 TYA	Sed Atk 211	R	16
95309	E566 TYA	Sed Atk 211	R	16
95311	E568 TYA	ERF 6x2	T	
95314	E656 XYC	Sed Atk 211	R	16
95315	E657 XYC	Sed Atk 211	R	16
95324	F93 BYD	Sed Atk 211	R	16
95348	DFJ 410Y	Dodge	R	13
95403	XYA 445S	ERF 4x2	T	
95413	DYB 317T	Sed Atk 200	R	16
95414	YYA 492S	Sed Atk 200	R	16
95436	DYB 327T	Sed Atk 200	R	16
95439	DYB 330T	Sed Atk 200	R	16
95445	FYA 296T	Sed Atk 200	R	16
95446	FYA 297T	Sed Atk 4x2	T	
95455	FYD 568T	Sed Atk 200	R	16
95461	EHT 376W	Bedford TL	R	12
95465	SYB 879W	Sed Atk 200	R	16
95466	SYB 886W	Dodge 50	R	5.6
95469	SYB 884W	Sed Atk 4x2	T	
95494	TYB 523W	Sed Atk 4x2	T	
95495	YYB 584X	Sed Atk 4x2	T	
95496	YYB 585X	Sed Atk 300	R	16
95497	YYB 586X	Sed Atk 300	R	16
95499	LYA 38V	Sed Atk 300	R	24

Vehicles based at Huddersfield

No	Reg no	Make/model Type,GVW*		
95252	JTC 146X	Bedford TL	R	12
95253	JTC 147X	Bedford TL	R	12
95254	LHY 574Y	Bedford TL	R	12
95255	A412 THW	Bedford TL	R	12
95256	A414 THW	Bedford TL	R	12
95264	GTW 669Y	Ford Cargo	R	11
95265	FYB 447Y	Ford Cargo	R	11
95266	FYB 446Y	Sed Atk 200	R	16
95267	FYB 453Y	Sed Atk 200	R	16
95268	FYB 454Y	Sed Atk 200	R	16
95275	A86 NYD	Sed Atk 6x2	T	
95276	A87 NYD	Sed Atk 6x2	T	
95277	A920 RHU	Sed Atk 300	R	16
95282	B139 VYD	Sed Atk 200	R	16
95283	B140 VYD	Sed Atk 200	R	16
95284	B141 VYD	Sed Atk 200	R	16
95292	B371 VTC	Bedford TL	R	12
95293	B372 VTC	Bedford TL	R	12
95294	D400 LYB	Bedford TL	R	12
95316	E658 XYC	Sed Atk 211	R	16
95319	F92 BYD	Sed Atk 211	R	16
95325	GYD 413K	ERF 4x2	T	
95326	F94 BYD	Sed Atk 211	R	16
95397	TYC 508R	Sed Atk 4x2	T	
95456	GHU 743X	Bedford CF	R	3.5
95471	CWS 907W	Bedford TL	R	12
95472	CWS 908W	Bedford TL	R	12
95473	DHY 416W	Bedford TL	R	12
95474	DHY 445W	Bedford TL	R	12
95475	EHT 377W	Bedford TL	R	12
95477	DHY 432W	Bedford TL	R	12
95478	DHY 433W	Bedford TL	R	12
95484	A359 TYD	Ford Escort van		
95485	TYB 520W	Sed Atk 300	R	16
95486	TYB 521W	Sed Atk 300	R	16
95493	YYB 583X	Sed Atk 300	R	16
95498	GHU 742X	Bedford CF	R	3.5

Vehicles based at Attleborough

No	Reg no	Make/model Type,GVW*		
95263	FYB 440Y	Sed Atk 6x2	T	
95270	ENE 383Y	Sed Atk 6x2	T	
95271	A80 NYD	ERF 6x2	T	
95273	A667 SHW	Bedford TL	R	16
95297	D398 LYB	Sed Atk 211	R	16
95312	E570 TYA	ERF	R	16
95313	E571 TYA	ERF	R	16
95327	F95 BYD	Sed Atk 211	R	16
95328	KYA 663K	ERF 4x2	T	
95329	TVX 651W	Ford	D	16
95330	TVX 652W	Ford	D	16
95331	TVX 653W	Ford	D	16
95346	TYB 388M	ERF 4x2	T	
95347	TYB 389M	ERF 4x2	T	
95380	YOG 746T	Ford Cargo	R	13
95382	C873 HTT	Dodge	R	13
95383	C874 HTT	Dodge	R	13
95437	DYB 328T	Sed Atk 200	R	16
95438	DYB 329T	Sed Atk 200	R	16
95459	YAE 927V	Bedford TK	R	12
95467	SYB 885W	Dodge 50	R	5.6
95468	SYB 877W	Sed Atk 4x2	T	
95476	DHY 431W	Bedford TL	R	12
95481	SYB 894W	Sed Atk 4x2	T	
95482	SYB 895W	Sed Atk 4x2	T	
95483	SYB 896W	Sed Atk 4x2	T	
95500	YYB 595X	Sed Atk 6x2	T	

Vehicles based at Cardiff

No	Reg no	Make/model Type,GVW*		
95257	B487 VHU	Sed Atk 201	R	16
95281	A417 THW	Bedford TL	R	12
95310	E567 TYA	Sed Atk 211	R	16
95317	F91 BYD	Sed Atk 211	R	16
95318	E659 XYC	Sed Atk 211	R	16
95349	DFJ 411Y	Dodge	R	13
95488	NEU 49Y	Bedford TL	R	7.5

Other vehicles

No	Reg no	Make/model Type,GVW*		
95320	UUO 851J	ERF	N	24
95322	SEU 120S	ERF	T	
95376	MYC 214P	Bedford	R	12
95377	VHW 89T	Bedford TL	R	12
95378	WHY 644T	Bedford TL	R	12
95379	D762 YMV	Bedford CF	R	3.5
95447	YOG 747T	Ford Cargo	R	13
95454	FYD 561T	Sed Atk 200	R	16
95458	XEU 699T	Bedford TK	R	12
95462	SYB 880W	Sed Atk 200	R	16
95470	SYB 887W	Dodge 100		

*Type: T, artic tractor unit; R, rigid; D, dray; N, tanker

12: GR-Stein Refractories Ltd

Not all own-account operators carry produce that is as well known as Babycham, in fact many carry items that most people know little about, and yet as a country we would have difficulty in prospering without their existence. GR-Stein Refractories Ltd is one such organization; having its centre in Sheffield, it is the largest manufacturer of refractory materials in the United Kingdom and now the second largest such producer in Europe.

If the term 'refractory' doesn't mean much to you, I should explain that GR-Stein's products are widely used throughout all the heat-using industries, particularly by the producers of iron and steel, cement, glass, non-ferrous metals and petrochemicals, as well as for power generation and incineration purposes. Describing them as brick producers might suggest an organization like The London Brick Company, but what sets GR-Stein's refractory bricks apart from the others is the great intensity of heat that they can withstand. One familiar application is in night storage heaters, where the bricks are used to absorb the heat very quickly and then slowly release it to create a home central-heating facility.

The company GR-Stein, as its name suggests, was in fact created as a result of a merger, in 1969, of the UK's two leading refractory producers, General Refractories Ltd of Sheffield and John G. Stein of Bonnybridge, Scotland. In 1970, GR-Stein became part of a larger group called Hepworth Ceramic Holdings PLC. Hepworths are well known as the leading producers of vitrified clay and plastic drainage systems as well as supplying other construction materials, industrial sands, minerals and resins. John G. Stein can trace their history back to 1887, but this chapter intends to concentrate on the activities of General Refractories Ltd and its transport division, which for a long time was called Genefax Transport, though that name is not currently used.

As a haulier, Genefax is probably one of the youngest featured in this book as, technically, it wasn't created until 1957. General Refractories Ltd, however, go back as far as 1913, when Mr F. Scott Russell set up the Kelham Island Firebrick Co. That company manufactured ground ganister, a stone material used for furnace linings, and also became a selling agent for foundry requisites and sand produced by other people. This agency aspect of Scott Russell's business was to be the key to General Refractories' development into a large conglomerate and also in essence how Genefax Transport was to be formed. The pattern that was followed in the business world was first to acquire selling rights for a particular manufacturer then, if his product was well accepted, to obtain a share in that business which would ultimately lead to total acquisition. To negotiate these transactions Scott Russell had set up a finance company called The British Refractories Corporation with its head office at Russell House, Adam Street, London.

The name General Refractories Company was adopted in 1920 to reflect the widening interests of Kelham Island Firebrick. The inventiveness of this concern was illustrated in the year of the General Strike, 1926, when in order to keep the kilns going, Midland Refractories Ltd, one of their subsidiaries, opened up a day-hole coal mine which came to be called Ambergate Colliery.

General Refractories Ltd was a further new name adopted in 1929 with the merger of the General Refractories Company and the Worksop Brick Company. Their main produce at this time were firebricks, silica bricks and sand, and they also made particularly hard bricks with a high chrome or magnesite content. The name 'Genefax' – an obvious abbreviation of General Refractories – was first coined in 1936 with the official opening of the Group's new headquarters in Sheffield, Genefax House.

F. Scott Russell officially retired in 1939 as chairman of the GR board, and the inheritance that he passed on to the following chairman, Sir Ronald Mathews, was a total of 36 different plants. Among them were nine firebrick works, plants that would make silica bricks, insulating bricks and even acid-resisting bricks. The sand aspect of the business at that time involved 12 moulding and silica sand quarries plus four ganister plants. After the war GR, like many others, assessed the direction they were going in and how best to bring their plant and equipment back to maximum performance. Transport eventually came under close scrutiny, which was to involve most importantly one Norman Maycock.

Norman could trace his connection with GR back as early as the 1930s period, first as an owner-driver hauling on a subcontract basis, and eventually growing to a fleet of about 20 in number which ran on 'C' hiring licences. All Maycock's vehicles were painted up in the colours of General Refractories, the line-up mostly being the lighter weight type of tipper based on Bedford, Dodge or even Vulcan chassis. Maycock got his first two Leyland vehicles – two eight-legger Octopus tippers – in 1954. It took some doing, getting a new vehicle, especially a Leyland, at that time; British Road Services, who were involved in an intensive restructuring programme, seemed to have first call on all their new lorries intended for the home market. But

Leyland did have a vested interest in Maycock's two tippers as they were to be worked on a dedicated sand contract feeding Leyland's own foundry. This first purchase was to set a pattern of Leyland allegiance which still sees the products of the Leyland-DAF marque predominate in the GR fleet.

What General Refractories did then, the direct opposite of the subcontract approach many own-account operations are considering these days, was to buy out Maycock's entire fleet of tippers and have him take over as Manager of the newly created Genefax Transport Ltd which was formed in 1957. True, GR had already been running some vehicles on their own account along with those of other subcontractors painted in their colours, but the Maycock acquisition started them along the path of being totally independent of the whims of outside hauliers.

Under the guidance of Maycock, Genefax Transport quickly expanded. Running on the 'C' carriers' licence – which meant you were restricted to carrying only your own products – was no problem to Genefax, that's all they wanted to do. The hauliers running on hire and reward traffic had to chase the elusive 'A' carriers' licences, and they met with little sympathy if they requested more from the Scrooge-like licensing authorities. But no apparent limit

Seen about May 1952, this fleet line-up belies the true ownership of the vehicles involved. Whilst the two new ERFs and two similar Atkinsons in the foreground were owned by General Refractories, the 20 remaining vehicles belonged to Norman Maycock. They were run in GR colours under a hiring carriers C licence and dedicated to GR traffic. The four Vulcans – next in line to the Atkinsons – were powered by the 4LW Gardner engine. All Maycock's vehicles were tippers although loading and unloading bricks was done by the traditional method of hand balling. Even back loads of clay were normally shovelled by hand onto the tipper's back.

These two Leyland Octopuses, seen at Ambergate in early 1954, were the first eight-wheelers run by Norman Maycock. They were also his first Leylands, the small Matlock operator getting preferential treatment as Leyland Motors had a declared interest in their use. Running from Chelford in Cheshire to the Leyland foundry, they carried two loads a day of special sand. Whilst 212 was driven by Alf Carson, Arthur Needum was given the keys of 222, which cost Maycock £3,000 to buy. Although having a top speed of only 28 mph, the Leyland was still too fast for the 20mph speed limit and Needum recalls getting booked and fined £1 for doing 25mph on the Prince of Wales road in Manchester.

Norman Maycock's vehicles weren't the only ones to run in the colours of General Refractories. TWT 256 was one of three lively AECs operated on contract by Marshalls of Bawtry. Seen here in about 1957, the dropsided-bodied Mercury normally ran hauling bricks from Worksop for use in the furnaces of South Wales. The vehicles of Marshall were eventually to be taken over by Maycock, just as he in turn was bought out to run under GR's ownership.

In October 1961 a total of six Leyland Octopus tippers in two convoys of three were the first Genefax vehicles to venture abroad on an experimental run betwen Glenboig Works in Scotland and GR's Seilles works in Belgium. Arthur Needum is seen rolling off the 'Cedric Ferry' at Antwerp after the 14-hour sea crossing from Tilbury. Genefax used 600-powered short-wheelbase tippers to try and keep the ferry costs down, the Leylands recording 8¾mpg for the 900-mile fully loaded round trip. Though the tippers ran loaded in both directions it was still deemed to be more cost-effective for the cargo to be carried by steamship out of Grangemouth. This experiment wasn't repeated until the mid-1970s. But driver Needum wasn't too displeased: his return ferry crossing coincided with the worst storm of the winter and took 36 hours to complete.

By 1961 the Genefax fleet had grown to 72 vehicles strong, 61 of which were from the Leyland Group. This Arthur Needum photograph shows a Super Comet six-wheeler which didn't come directly off the Leyland production line. To increase capacity and allow 20-ton gross loadings, Genefax took the four-wheeled chassis to York's at Corby who grafted on the rear trailing axle. Seen in 1959 at the Leyland plant, driver Bill Spray is climbing aboard the 375-powered tipper about to drop his load of sand. Spray was one of Maycock's first drivers and worked for the company for about 40 years.

Up until the late 1960s, the multi-wheeled rigid tipper was the standard Genefax machine, with some eight-wheelers even hauling four-wheeled drawbar trailers. VWE 848F was Leyland chassis number 800765 and was received in chassis and cab form by Genefax on April 8, 1968. Three days later it went to Kay's for fitment of the tipping gear and body, being delivered back to the Ambergate depot on May 22, 1968. Ray Smith was the regular driver.

Above: this Scammell Trunker II was a rare tanker in the Genefax fleet, being bought to haul fuel oil from Immingham to the GR works at Worksop. This Arthur Needum photograph shows the vehicle on the wash at Ambergate works on the day of delivery, July 26, 1968. The vehicle wasn't registered until the next month when it was given the mark WWE 388G. Chassis number WHV 11032 had a rather inauspicious start and suffered a fan through the radiator on October 11, 1968. 20 years on, the tanker is still in one piece waiting at the Bawtry works for further utilization. The five-axle Trunker outfit was one of the few artics that could run at the newly introduced 32 tons weight band when the weight limit was linked to a strange requirement for outer-axle spread whilst still remaining in a restricted overall length limit. Below: Genefax only ran three or four of the troublesome fixed-head 500-series-engined Leyland Buffalos. WWA 26S was chassis number 7801513, delivered to the operator on June 1, 1978. Its tare weight was recorded as being 11½ tons. It is coupled to what became a trade mark of the Genefax fleet, a low-height triple-dropside tandem-axle tipping semi-trailer. Built in light alloy by Cravens Homalloy, these trailers were particularly strong to withstand GR's heavy traffic. The dropsides allowed for normal side-loading of palleted traffic yet when in the upright position offered a tight enough fit to contain specialized dense materials.

was put in the way of own-account requests for more 'C' licences.

As Genefax expanded, the allegiance to Leyland grew stronger, not only to the Lancashire-built vehicles but also to those made by other members of the expanding Leyland empire, Scammell at Watford, Albion at Scotstoun and eventually Guy in Wolverhampton. Whilst Sheffield was the heart of the General Refractories organization, Genefax Transport had their resources spread around with depots at Deepcar, Bawtry, Ambergate in Derbyshire and Worksop, the latter one of the main centres from which vehicles ran nationwide and, after 1961, even across to the Continent.

Talking about that experiment nearly 30 years on, it may not sound very exciting but in essence the Genefax men were breaking new ground. General Refractories had owned a subsidiary in Belgium since 1936, but prior to '61, cargo between the UK and Belgium had always been carried across the water in small coasters, with two different lorries being utilized for the road movements at either end. More than 10 years before we actually joined – in 1973 – the talk was already all about our entry into the Common Market and how industry had to adapt to the new challenge by increasing its flexibility with the onset of more competition. To Genefax it was more simply an exercise in costing and for the experiment two sets of three Leyland Octopus tippers were used. Their departure from the Glenboig works in Scotland was staggered to ensure the vehicles weren't out of UK service for too long a period.

It was a 400-mile run down to Tilbury from Glenboig, with their destination at Seilles being about 140 miles from the ferry's docking point at Antwerp. Ferry traffic was very much in its infancy early in the 1960s and today a shorter, less expensive Dover-Ostend route might well have been taken. As it was, although the transport operation proved a success, the sheer cost, including the heavy ferry charges at that time, meant it was cheaper to freight the cargo by ship even though it had to be loaded and unloaded twice and use two different roadgoing cargo carriers. Whilst guaranteed delivery was promised in a far quicker fashion using a driver-accompanied lorry for the entire journey, when the traffic wasn't urgent the increase in basic costings seemed difficult to justify.

Back in the UK, the cargo being hauled on Genefax's vehicles was destined for a significant change. Whilst GR had not gone in for absorbing as many companies as they had done prior to World War 2, a signifigant tie-up in 1963 was that with British Industrial Sand. By November 1964, BIS was to take over all the sand sales and production from the previous General Refractories portfolio, meaning the Genefax vehicles stopped carrying that type of traffic. What was left for them to haul was continuing to expand in volume, the one common denominator being that it was always going to be heavy. So whilst the eight-wheeled rigid had been the leader of the Genefax fleet since 1952, once the changing legislation in the mid-1960s gave the artics a bigger potential payload margin, Genefax were quick to change over to the 32-ton train-weight articulated outfits.

A pattern of semi-trailer was adopted fairly soon that was to stay in use right up to the next change in weight bands that occurred in May 1983. This standard Genefax semi-trailer could be spotted a mile off, not just because it was a tipper, but because it had a triple-dropside body which would have looked more at home on an old-fashioned eight-legger. Whilst a normal tipper always tended to have rather high sides, the Genefax sideboards were hardly more than a couple of feet. This was the clue to the fact that the Genefax outfit was very much a dual-purpose workhorse, capable of carrying heavyweight bricks on the outward journey and heavy stone, dolomite or other raw materials back to the producing plants around Sheffield and Worksop. The tipping body ensured swift unloading of this inward-bound traffic, whilst the strength of the Genefax trailers was in their flooring of 1/4in-thick solid steel plate.

The size of the Genefax fleet was to peak about 1973 at around 110 vehicles. By then the company had merged both with John G. Stein and Hepworth Iron Co Ltd. The period

General Refractories Ltd was to receive the Queen's award for achievements in the export trade. Currently its specialist materials are moved like most other exports by container, although the small size of this ACE carrier gives some indication of the heavy weight of its contents. Pictured in the Manuel Works, Linlithgow, the GR-Stein Marathon is providing traction for this ACE semi-trailer carrying a GR-made cargo. Genefax were to get good service from their many Leyland Marathons, the last of which ran until 1988.

By 1988 the fleet had seen a sharp reduction to less than a third of the 110 vehicles run in the mid-1970s. Leyland 6x2 Roadtrains dominated with 17 of these Cummins-powered units in use. The vast majority were powered by the 14-litre Cummins E320 but one exception was D438 SWE, chassis number 71914, which was powered by the L10 Cummins 290bhp version, going into service on July 1, 1987. On average the L10 was returning 7.88mpg running 1,500 miles per week, a shade less than the more favoured E320. The Task semi-trailer was also a change in direction for Genefax, the curtainsiders giving better versatility especially when a variety of third-party cargo was being hauled.

also saw Bob Exley take over as head of Genefax from Norman Maycock in 1975. The rigours of recession that were to hit most of industry at the turn of that decade didn't miss out GR-Stein. At that point the overheads of such a large transport fleet became abundantly clear, especially when there were plenty of hauliers around keen to shave their rates down in order to keep their vehicles earning. The order came down from the Board that the fleet had to be reduced and today it stands close to the 30 mark.

Genefax Transport as a name was dropped at the start of 1988, the haulage entity now referred to simply as the Transport Division of its parent, GR-Stein. Centre of its operations is at the company's Austerfield plant near Bawtry, although five vehicles are based in Scotland, running out of the Manuel works at Linlithgow. This particular site operates a large firebrick, high-alumina brick and monolithic plant.

It wasn't only the recession that prompted the retraction of the Genefax fleet, there were also major changes that affected the international transportation of goods. It is containers that have transformed this line of work, with the cargo being loaded directly into the large steel boxes before

it leaves the manufacturer's plant, so saving on massive labour charges for rehandling. This sort of traffic was then to be moved by the container operator's own hauliers and as GR-Stein were to export over 40% of their total sales, it was a very big slice of traffic that was involved.

For UK haulage, the fleet of GR-Stein is now solidly into 38-tonne artics. Initially they chose a 2+3 combination headed up by the Rolls-Royce-powered Leyland Roadtrain but after Bob Exley had tried out the 6 × 2 Scammell-built version of the Leyland-badged 38-tonner, this was to be the type of workhorse that was adopted. The trailers too have seen a variation from the standard 40ft flat and the tipping triple-dropsider, for now curtainsiders are regularly being introduced. As well as being a lot easier to secure than the old rope and sheet method, the new load-carrier makes the GR-Stein vehicle more adaptable to carry a wider range of traffic. The change over to operators licensing way back in 1968 means the Transport Division can carry third-party traffic as and when required, which makes them a fitter albeit a leaner organization ready to haul for their parent as the 1990s approach. It may not be as big a fleet as it was 20 years ago but it is still a force to be reckoned with.

Fleet List
GR-STEIN REFRACTORIES LTD

Reg no	Make and type	Engine	Registered	Chassis no
KWB 115P	Scammell Routeman	680	1/08/75	WHV60065/001
SYV 470S	Bedford		3/10/77	GW111014
DKY 339V	Scammell Crusader	Rolls-Royce	1/09/79	59495
TWB 263Y	Leyland Roadtrain (2)	Rolls-Royce 265	1/09/82	8231274
TAK 330Y	Leyland Roadtrain (2)	Rolls-Royce 265	1/10/82	8231711
TAK 331Y	Leyland Roadtrain (2)	Rolls-Royce 265	1/10/82	8231594
A655 XWF	Leyland Roadtrain (2)	Rolls-Royce 290	1/08/83	35562
A761 XHE	Leyland Roadtrain (2)	Rolls-Royce 290	6/09/83	32482
A327 WWJ	Leyland Roadtrain (3)	Cummins NTE 320	1/01/84	76148
A377 AWF	Leyland Roadtrain (3)	Cummins NTE 320	1/03/84	76293
A378 AWF	Leyland Roadtrain (3)	Cummins NTE 320	1/03/84	76295
A504 AAK	Leyland Roadtrain (3)	Cummins NTE 320	1/06/84	76303
B798 EDT	Leyland Roadtrain (3)	Cummins NTE 320	1/02/85	76660
B799 EDT	Leyland Roadtrain (3)	Cummins NTE 320	1/02/85	76656
B704 FKW	Leyland Roadtrain (3)	Cummins NTE 320	15/05/85	76848
B680 GWA	Leyland Roadtrain (3)	Cummins NTE 320	1/06/85	76845
C970 HKU	Leyland Roadtrain (3)	Cummins NTE 320	1/09/85	76934
C971 HKU	Leyland Roadtrain (3)	Cummins NTE 320	1/09/85	76929
C139 KWA	Leyland Roadtrain (3)	Cummins NTE 320	1/01/86	70128
C920 LHE	Leyland Roadtrain (3)	Cummins NTE 320	2/05/86	70122
D487 PET	Austin Maestro 700 Van		12/12/86	AM424554
D296 NWB	Leyland Roadtrain (3)	Cummins L10 290	19/01/87	70846
D826 DVN	DAF (3)	DAF DKXE1160	1/02/87	291315
D438 SWE	Leyland Roadtrain (3)	Cummins L10 290	1/07/87	71914
D654 FDC	DAF (3)	DAF 2800	1/07/87	296219
D439 SWE	Leyland 2-axle rigid	Leyland 422	10/07/87	60659
E649 KVN	Leyland Roadtrain (3)	Cummins NTE 320	1/01/88	71679
E650 KVN	Leyland Roadtrain (3)	Cummins NTE 320	1/01/88	71987
E651 KVN	Leyland Roadtrain (3)	Cummins NTE 320	1/01/88	71978
E652 KVN	Leyland Roadtrain (3)	Cummins NTE 320	1/01/88	71920

13: Siddle C. Cook Ltd

Discuss the Classic Hauliers of yesteryear and it isn't long before the name of Siddle C. Cook is brought into the conversation. The picture conjured up in the mind's eye of an old red Scammell hauling massive lengths of steel seems so clear and distinct that you can almost smell the fumes from its Gardner engine and feel the heat from its brakes as it claws its way ever onward, for both Scammells and steel were a Cook trademark, especially in their heyday in the 1950s and '60s.

Although Siddle was to ensure that the Cook name became synonymous with flair, imagination and a sheer gutsy way of tackling whatever came their way, it was his father, Thomas, who started the Cooks off in transport back in 1891. At the time he was actually a farm labourer but, passing the time in a local hostelry, he heard the talk around him about the local store horse that was going to be put down. The Co-operative Wholesale Society couldn't deny that it was as strong as they came but they just couldn't live with its antics. It had already turned over five cart-loads of groceries and none of the delivery men could handle it, it was quite a beast. The Co-op had tried to sell it and pitched the price very low at 3/6d (17½p) but even that didn't tempt anyone until Tom Cook decided to invest all he possessed. In fact, he was a shilling short and had to borrow that 5p for a week to make the purchase.

To go with the horse, Tom was able to borrow a set of harnesses and also made use of a cart belonging to the farmer he worked for. This was done on the understanding that on each day he borrowed the cart, he would spread a load of manure on the fields at night as payment. What the horse and cart was to earn its keep at was a fairly regular routine. At three farthings a time, which is about a quarter of a decimal penny, Cook's contract was to empty the ash closet toilets for the long lines of back-to-back houses that were characteristic of the mining community of north-west Durham. It may not have been a job that everyone wanted, but it was a service greatly appreciated in the days prior to the flushing convenience of modern sanitation.

You could just about call it a haulage business – Cook certainly developed it into one and by the 1930s not only had he got into motor lorries, he was running three vehicles on 'A' licences, with a further two on contract 'A' by the time war broke out in 1939. There was nothing particularly flash in the line-up; a Foden registered AUP 952, a Bedford, BPT 624 and a bonneted Leyland, WV 1633, were the three open 'A' vehicles and although Tom's son Siddle was to drive them all at one time or another, it was the bonneted Leyland which he was normally seen at work with.

During the mid-1930s, the Leyland was run as a four-wheeled tipper carrying tarmac roadstone out of Crookhall near Consett. Both the vehicle and its driver turned people's heads, the polished Leyland because it only had a one-door cab entrance and Siddle Cook because of his choice of dress. Burnished leather gaiters were worn over highly polished boots with a railwayman type cheese-cutter hat almost a permanent fixture on his head – quite a turn out for a tipper driver of the '30s.

With rate-cutting getting out of hand at Crookhall, Cooks next turned to timber work for Hunnicliffe's and, like the Sunter brothers of Northallerton, they converted their rigid four-wheelers into crude but very effective long artics. This proved to be the major turning point in the Cooks' transport fortunes, although Thomas wasn't to see the concept develop for he died in 1942.

Although Siddle was only one of a big family, he held the reins of the business during the wartime years. In 1945, the various brothers set out in their own directions with Siddle forming his own well known limited company with three heavyweight artics. This Cook fleet of the late 1940s was based on ERF four-wheeled tractors, with bigger Foden six-wheeled units for the heavier work. Following the take-over of smaller operations like J.E. Hirst of Tow Law,

Although Thomas Cook had started in horse-and-cart haulage as far back as 1891, it wasn't until the twilight of his life that he started to run long-length outfits. The bonneted Leyland depicted on this faded but atmospheric postcard had an unladen weight of 4¾tons and originally started life as a four-wheeled tipper but Cook converted it for artic use, the standard longer wheelbase giving far more stability when 80ft-long trees had to be hauled. Siddle Cook is seen standing on top of this typical load with his brother Septimus to the right of shot and brother-in-law Jim Bartrop on the left. Permitted top speed of the outfit was 16mph.

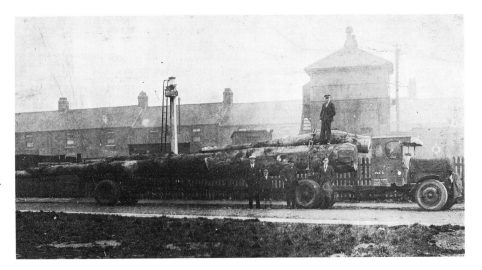

mainly to acquire the vehicles' carrier licences, the expanding fleet forced Cook to consider moving on from his cramped premises at 7, Taylor Street in Consett. He had paid £90 for an old stone quarry in Sherburn Terrace back in 1942, but it took ten persistent years before planning permission was obtained for the new depot.

On May 3, 1951, the British Transport Commission's programme of nationalization reached Consett, with eleven of Siddle's fleet being taken to form the British Road Services unit D480. Not a total buy-out, for Cook was left with three low-loaders and one artic, deemed as heavy haulage vehicles and thus exempted from compulsory purchase. The absence of any such nationalization of passenger transport allowed Cooks to buy and operate six buses which incuded the first luxury Guy Arab to be fitted with the Gardner 6HLW engine. It was always Siddle's plan that his transport interests should eventually pass on to his daughter and two sons. The scheme was that daughter Pauline was to inherit the coach side of the business, but friction with drivers over rates of pay for weekend and late-

night working irritated Siddle and within a couple of years the buses were all sold.

This move coincided with denationalization in 1953 as the grip of British Road Services was loosened a little. Cook started to invest back amongst his favoured ERF and Foden heavyweights, although it cost him £13,000 to buy the massive steel work for the large-span garage to be erected in Sherburn Terrace. In the era of the ration book, such a purchase was only permitted by first obtaining a Certificate of Need through the Ministry of Supply, a regular headache required even for buying things like new tyres and lorry spare parts.

Getting round administrative problems like this was never to be one of Siddle's favourite pastimes but where the man was to shine was in conceiving ideas for solving particular transport problems. Many's the night he would spend tossing and turning in bed as his mind wrestled with how his limited amount of equipment could carry the next problem of a load. Daybreak would normally bring a solution which would be drawn on the garage floor in chalk

Siddle Cook formed his own limited company in 1945 operating from premises situated at 7, Taylor Street, Consett. This ERF artic low-loader, believed to be EUP 766, is seen in Taylor Street in about 1948. The saddle-tank locomotive is one of four similar loads that Cooks hauled from Stanhope into the Consett Iron Company works around that time. The driver's mate is Bobby Hodgson, whilst the driver is Harold 'Butch' Warrington who was later to leave Cooks to drive for Wrekin Roadways.

107

Although Siddle Cook ran private hire buses during the period from 1951 to 1953 whilst the majority of his lorries were nationalized, he first became involved in private hire work as early as 1946, when Cooks were given the job of ferrying workmen from the Newcastle and Sunderland areas up to the Consett Iron works. Offered for charter to more discerning passengers, the OB Bedford, seen here, fitted with a Duple Vista body, was registered KUP 711. This vehicle was bought new in May 1950 but sold to the General Omnibus Service Co when Cooks decided to go back into lorries exclusively in July 1953.

so that his engineers would have some idea what Cooky had come up with. Siddle always said in hindsight that he wished he had gone into trailer manufacture rather than staying in haulage. His inspired creations were also studied by some of the big names in trailer building who weren't averse to intercepting Cooks outfits out on the road. While they paid for the driver's breakfast, time was allowed for them to photograph and study the load carrier for subsequent guidance in their own building programme.

Hauling these trailers had weaned Siddle off Fodens and once Scammell produced stronger shaft-drive rather than chain-drive tractors, these bonneted powerhouses took over

occupancy of the Consett depot. The colour of the units had originally been red but Siddle had a phase of painting them cream with red lettering. This paint scheme didn't last long before the red was reinstated, Cook saying that he preferred it that his vehicles remained more inconspicuous. How he expected this with 80ft lengths of steel being hauled wasn't really clear.

Another distinctive feature of the newly bought Cook Scammells was that they always tended to be registered with their numbers finishing in 00. It thus became difficult to differentiate say between RPT 400, TPT 600, XPT 600 or even RPT 800, but whether or not this was a ploy

A far classier and more luxurious coach was this Guy Arab fitted with Burlingham Seagull bodywork. Siddle recalls paying £7,328 for this vehicle, which was £28 more than he was to pay for his big 6x6 Scammell Constructor which he bought new in 1955. This Guy was reportedly the first coach to have the horizontal or 'flat' version of the six-cylinder Gardner engine which was called the 6HLW. Coming new to Consett in March 1952, it was sold on to Graham Brothers of Winlaton Mill in August 1953 along with the three sets of passenger head-rest covers made specially for the vehicle by Siddle's wife.

Following the onset of denationalization in 1953, Cook was to buy back into general haulage although he was already accepted as one of the growing specialist band of heavyweight and abnormal-load carriers. About 1954 he was still placing faith in six-wheeled Fodens to move some phenomenal loads such as this impressive 120ft-long crane girder. Weighing in at around 60 tons, the 10ft-wide load was made at Palmers of Hebburn then transported by Cooks to Hawarden Bridge. Driving JUP 826 was Marshall Eglon, whilst Harry Bolam was driving the double-heading MPT 527. The latter powerhouse Foden had just been bought from Crook & Willington Carriers and still sports their own specially built crew-cab. At the time of writing, Harry Bolam is still driving trucks for Wrights of Tow Law who run ERF low-loaders.

MPT 527 was the leading light when Cooks moved what was arguably their most impressive load, seen here passing through the centre of Darlington. At 10ft wide and 51 tons in weight it may not seem a great deal to write home about, but when the length of the vessel is 127ft and it is road-hauled all the way from Newcastle to Shellhaven in Essex, it must reflect greatly on the skill of driver George 'Jock' Walker. No modern steerable bogie was available for the Cook men, just a solid lump of a 16-wheeler, made by Eric Temperley, a burner from Consett Iron Company, that probably would have taken most of the weight not just some of it. Prior to the job, the crew cab of MPT 527 was cut off by the carpenter at Cooks so that the vessel had more room to swing forward of the tractor-mounted bolster. It took four days of delicate work to load the column, and a week prior to that was spent working out where to locate the rear bogie. It was eventually placed at 80ft or about two-thirds of the way down the load.

deliberately to unsettle the enforcement brigade isn't immediately admitted by Siddle.

In 1955 Siddle bought a version of the biggest Scammell then being made, a Rolls-Royce-powered 6x6 Constructor. At £7,300, SPT 600 was quite a commitment. It was the strongest tractor yet to come to Consett, although in February of the following year it was simply used as a back-up when Cooks were involved in moving probably the most awkward load they were ever asked to deliver.

At 51 tons, the splitter column wasn't excessively heavy but finding a route from Newcastle to Shellhaven in Essex for something 127 feet in length, on the archaic road system of 30 years ago, was a nightmare. Such a special-order load should really have gone by ship but, with nothing suitable available at sea, the task was taken on by driver George 'Jock' Walker and his five-man crew. Harry Maggs, driving the big Constructor, was in attendance but Jock had Foden MPT 527 carrying the load at one end and a huge sixteen-tyred non-steerable bogie supporting at the other end. The bogie was actually the running gear from a tank transporting

Above: by 1957, the date of this Arthur Philipson photograph, the four-wheeled Scammell tractor unit in varying states of maturity was beginning to dominate the Cook fleet. Driving these machines was not everyone's cup of tea although Cooks were still to get many enquiries from potential employees. 'Can you drive a Scammell?' Siddle used to ask and, if the reply seemed too confident or cocky, he would ask the applicant to drive round the yard an old unit which wasn't fitted with the hefty steel gate round the gear lever; this meant in essence that if you didn't know your way blindfold round the Scammell you just didn't have the slightest chance of changing gear correctly. One unusual vehicle not seen in this partial fleet shot was a 4x4 Latil used as a recovery and winching tractor, the original petrol engine being replaced by Cooks with a Gardner 5LW. Below: by 1958 the last two Fodens in the Cook fleet were not long from being disposed of. MPT 527 became part of the Cook legend but less well known was UUP 500 which was in fact built at Sherburn Terrace. Most of the bits for this six-wheeler had come off another Foden that had been written off after a runaway; its driver, 'The Black Knight', had jumped out just before the vehicle crashed. With Foden refusing to sell Cooks a complete new chassis for the vehicle, Siddle bought one frame member at a time and slowly reconstructed it that way. It was in fact fitted into the vehicle the wrong way round – the front to the rear – Cook feeling it would be stronger in that form. The cab, looking like a normal S18, was built by Cooks carpenter, Frank Whitton. Another memorable vehicle in the centre of the picture is number 63, OXJ 637, one of the two box tractors bought from Diamond Transport.

Above: the old red Scammell became the standard Cook workhorse, though driver Jock Gallagher's VPT 800 was a fairly modern version, being bought new in 1956. Allocated the fleet number 47, the Scammell had the almost standard Cook engine, the Gardner 6LW. Although Cooks seemed to have an abundance of low-loaders, there were not always enough: Jock Walker tells the story of an urgent load requiring collection at Coles Cranes, Sunderland, when the only working Scammell in the yard was a vehicle with no cab fitted. Jock was ordered by the old man to set out for Coles perched on a wooden box on the exposed chassis, but he had only managed 10 miles when he was stopped by the law and told it was best to go straight back to Consett. Below: Cooks first started running Guys as early as 1956 but it wasn't until the 1959-61 era that they were bought in abundance. The Invincible seen in this Arthur Philipson shot was a modern-looking vehicle at the time and was to be well liked both by the company and the drivers. 100 GPT was the second big 6x4 unit, coming to Consett in 1960 and following 400 EPT, new the previous year. Both the vehicles had the Gardner 6LX engine and were used respectively by drivers Harry Bolam and Charlie Burnell. Whilst these two may have been tremendous steel shifters, the real powerhouse among the Invincibles in the fleet was 2100 PT, Billy Thompson's 6x4 wagon which had the Rolls-Royce 12.17 engine and ZF 12-speed gearbox.

Siddle himself is seen here in front of his centre of operations on Sherburn Terrace, Consett. The photograph dates from 1960 when 100 JPT had just been delivered new from Watford. This was the first of only two of this type of Highwayman run by Cooks, the second one being 8700 UP, which was to have the fleet number 116. Both tractors were fitted with the more powerful Gardner 6LX 150bhp engine.

For sheer charisma and style, the batch of four bonneted Leylands that Cooks bought during 1960 took some beating. There were two Super Beavers – 9800 UP and 9900 UP – whilst the sister vehicle to this Super Hippo was 9100 UP. Billy Gilligan was to be the driver of this Leyland which had the fleet number 103. It is shown without its famous radiator badge, 'El Camion Ingles', affixed mainly to show that it was an export version and should really have gone abroad to sunnier climes. The vehicle is seen, soon after delivery, in the Tallington works of Dow Mac.

trailer supporting a swiveling bolster with two locking pins to hold the bolster and load aligned when running straight ahead. When manoeuvring round the multitude of bends and roundabouts involved in the 350-mile haul, the Scammell Constructor was hung on either behind or at the side of the load. With the locking pins on the bolster removed, the Scammell would drag the bogie round with a wire hawser to point roughly in the desired direction.

With so much power under his foot, Harry Maggs was keen to double-head the Foden but only once did Jock Walker allow him to do it and 30 years or so later he still shudders at the scare that Harry gave him. Jock sensed that Harry had no fear and even though he recalls having the footbrake pedal on the Foden pushed through the floor, the Scammell was pulling it and the load well up to 30mph as they bisected Welwyn Garden City. Jock eventually delivered this load quite safely – perhaps the high point of the trip was the hour spent getting round Gantshill roundabout in north-east London.

The Constructor, bought as a ballast-box tractor, was

never fully utilized by Cooks in this drawbar fashion. Siddle hated the idea of carrying 20 tons of dead ballast weight in the box on the back of the Constructor simply to ensure traction of the rear drive wheels. He conceived at that time an idea to fit a 10-ton combined engine and generator in the ballast box and use the power generated to drive electric motors which would be hub-mounted throughout the trailer. The idea was never to bear fruit; instead, converting the big Scammell into a massive artic made it more useful and meant it hardly ever stopped running.

The smaller Scammells were also run as artics with the exception of VTC 649 and OXJ 637, two box tractors bought from Diamond Transport of Ashton-under-Lyne specifically for their 'A' carriers' licences. Rated only as 25-tonners, they were worked really hard. Driver Joe Corbett can recall hauling 39-ton steel rolls from Glasgow to South Wales using one of these little Scammells and that included tackling the notorious A6 at Shap without assistance.

Siddle paid good rates to his staff but if he sensed anyone was slacking or not giving of their best he could snarl like a terrier and make their life hell. As time went by he rewarded his drivers with more modern vehicles, and the 1960s saw many Guy tractors being bought. Apart from the Rolls-powered 2100 PT, the Gardner engine was virtually a standard Cook requirement. Although these Guy Invincibles had a classic look to them, they were beaten for sheer charisma by a quartet of bonneted Leylands that came to Consett in mid-1963. Intended originally to be exported to sunnier climes, the two Super Beavers and two Super Hippos were real head-turners.

However hardly had these big Leylands begun to get into their stride, when Siddle took the decision to sell the fleet as a going concern to the Tayforth Group. The reasons behind the decision involved some personal considerations and some practical ones but, after a lot of sleepless nights, July 3, 1964, saw the announcement that Tayforth had acquired Siddle C. Cook Ltd in a £225,000 cash deal. With Geoff Cook staying on as a manager nothing much seemed to change, the only small difference being a Tayforth motif painted discreetly on the front of the red Cook wagons.

The late 1960s brought the introduction of the plating and testing regulations and the Scammells of old were swept away. In their place came Trunker 2s, Handymen, AEC Mandators, Atkinson four and six-wheelers and perhaps a more normal look to the Cook fleet. Geoff Cook ensured that heavy haulage could still be tackled with the replacement of the ageing Constructor by a 240-ton Contractor, XUP 999F, but shortly after this, he too left to set up on his own in general haulage.

Siddle and his younger son Raymond had moved into the caravan manufacturing business, and the name they adopted for this new breed of van was Elddis, a title that Geoff Cook also used for his newly formed transport company. Cook followers will realize that Elddis is simply Siddle spelt backwards and, with the eventual disappearance of the red-liveried Cooks vehicles into a reshuffled Tayforth/NFC organisation, the name is all that remains of the Siddle Coderling Cook legend.

```
Fleet List
SIDDLE C. COOK LTD

Vehicles in use about 1962

No   Reg no    Make and type
 1   UUP 500   Foden 6x4 artic unit
 4   XPT 600   Scammell 4x2 artic unit
 6   TPT 600   Scammell 4x2 artic unit
 8   RPT 400   Scammell 4x2 artic unit
 9   MPT 527   Foden 6x4 artic unit
21   DUU 339   Scammell 4x2 artic unit
28   RPT 800   Scammell 4x2 artic unit
30   SPT 600   Scammell 6x6 Constructor
33   RUP 900   Scammell 4x4 Mountaineer
36   EYY 590   Scammell 4x2 artic unit
44   VPT 500   Scammell Rigid 8 platform
47   VPT 800   Scammell 4x2 artic unit
49   GXV 370   Scammell 4x2 artic unit
56   XPT 900   Guy 4x2 artic unit
58   YPT 800   Guy platform eight-wheeler
59   YPT 900   Guy platform eight-wheeler
62   VTC 649   Scammell 4x2 box tractor
63   OXJ 637   Scammell 4x2 box tractor
65   200 APT   Scammell 4x4 Mountaineer
72   NTY 306   Scammell 4x2 artic unit
76   300 EPT   Guy platform four-wheeler
77   700 EPT   Guy platform four-wheeler

No    Reg no     Make and type
78    400 EPT    Guy 6x4 artic unit
79    700 EUP    Albion Chieftain platform
                              four-wheeler
82    100 GPT    Guy 6x4 artic unit
83    600 HPT    Guy 4x2 artic unit
84    700 HPT    Guy 4x2 artic unit
85    100 HUP    Guy 4x2 artic unit
86    500 HUP    Guy 4x2 artic unit
87    100 JPT    Scammell 4x2 artic unit
88    500 JUP    Guy 4x2 artic unit
89    1300 PT    Guy 4x2 artic unit
90    JXE 752    Scammell 4x2 artic unit
91    2100 PT    Guy 6x4 artic unit
92    2600 PT    Guy Warrior Light 8 platform
93    2900 PT    Leyland Beaver 4x2 artic unit
94    3400 PT    Guy 4x2 artic unit
95    MLE 882    Scammell 4x2 artic unit
96    4100 PT    Scammell four-wheeled tractor
97    KGW 351    Scammell 4x2 artic unit
99    6300 PT    Guy 4x2 artic unit
100   5700 PT    Scammell Handyman 4x2 artic
101   6400 PT    AEC Mammoth Major platform
```

14: Crook & Willington Carriers Ltd

Whilst Cooks may have been one of the big head-turners of yesteryear, a company which rivalled them both in flair and ability if not in size was Crook & Willington Carriers, who based their heavy haulage operations at Bishop Auckland in County Durham. Half-a-dozen low-loaders was never going to worry the likes of the mighty Pickfords but Crook & Willington established a niche for themselves especially in the movement of battle tanks for the Ministry of Supply, a big turn-round from what the company had originally set out to do.

It was in 1939 that Geoff Smith of 6, The Green, Hunwick decided to go into transport. He was already running a garage and, along with general car repairs, he operated a hearse, a line of funeral cars and an ambulance. The two lorries he put to work mainly hauled out of Doctor's Gate quarry near Wolsingham, hauling ganister ten miles to meet the special demands of West Hunwick Silicas near Crook. Named after two adjoining towns in western Durham, Crook & Willington Carriers had a rather grand-sounding ring to its title. The two vehicles it operated were a complete contrast to that image; they were an International four-wheeled tipper registered EPT 237 and a four-wheeler of rather indeterminate make. This vehicle had started life as a passenger-carrying bus, but shorn of its seats and fittings, the platform body had flimsy dropsides and no form of tipping gear to unload its cargo.

Joe Elliott was not a man to be put off by appearances, as driver Tony Swann can recall, for he was stopped one day by Joe so that he could inspect his vehicle. It seems an odd way to do business but a week later Geoff Smith was to announce to his drivers that he had sold the haulage side of his business to Elliott for £888 17s 9d. Prior to his step into haulage, Joe Elliott had specialized in public works and other site constructions. Laying water mains was his speciality and initially the vehicles worked in that vein before being requisitioned for airfield construction. The converted

bus had been quickly disposed of and in its place came an Austin three-way tipper, LME 985.

With the end of the war approaching in 1945, the International was sold and replaced by FUP 115, a sparkling new Scammell articulated low-loader. It worked very closely with the Austin tipper: the Scammell would haul, say, a bulldozer, whilst the Austin would carry the scraper trailer that was towed by the bulldozers to clear sites.

Rated as just a 20-tonner, the shaft-drive Scammell was worked hard as Crook & Willington began to be requested to move abnormal loads a lot heavier than the normal plant work. Elliott looked round to strengthen his fleet but found little on the market to suit. He wanted a strong six-wheeled artic tractor unit that could also run in ballasted form and, as Scammell didn't have anything in this range to suit, Fodens were approached to build one of their made-to-measure specials. MPT 527 came to County Durham in August 1951, the FGTU 6/30 unit having the Gardner 6LW engine, 8-speed gearbox and hand-operated reduction hubs on its double-drive bogie. One mod soon fitted by C & W to the Foden was a crew cab compartment needed to accommodate both the gang men used on installation work and also the growing number of statutory attendants or mates that the law said you needed to carry when hauling long or wide loads.

Less than a year after taking delivery of this first Foden, Elliott ordered NUP 234, something so special that Fodens used it as a Motor Show exhibit in late 1952. Chassis number 34508 was an FGTU 8/80, fitted with a massive 8-cylinder Gardner engine, 12-speed epicyclic gearbox, double-reduction hubs and having an ability to climb house ends. It retained its Motor Show adornments, a white steering wheel and a chromium-plated gear lever, and leading driver Baldwin warmed to his new vehicle – well, anyone would have, mainly because of the terrific heat generated by that eight-pot Gardner.

FUP 115 was bought new from Scammells in March 1945 and was originally coupled with a four-in-line Scammell low-loading semi-trailer. However for moving a number of these chimney sections from Peers of Bolton to East Linton near Edinburgh, a 40ft step-frame semi-trailer belonging to Elliotts of York was utilized, not a great deal of weight for the shaft-drive tractor unit that was officially rated as a 20-tonner and had the Gardner 6LW engine and six-speed gearbox. The first crew of the vehicle were Arthur Baldwin and Jimmy Graver who kept it in such a pristine condition that the manufacturer gave them ten shillings each (50p) when they took it back to Watford for its first repair.

Second in the pecking order of drivers was Tony Swann who had been quite happy getting Arthur's hand-me-downs, but in May 1954 he got PPT 672, a new vehicle which was to make him a legend amongst his own work mates. With exposed radiator and similar crew cab, the new Foden looked identical to its stable-mate – chromium gear lever apart – but fired into life the later six-wheeler screamed out its big difference in typical two-stroke fashion. The Foden engine it was fitted with was like a firey stallion compared to the cart-horse Gardners, but like any thoroughbred it needed an understanding jockey to get the best from it. Tony Swann was a man gifted with both the ear to detect the peak in performance and the feel to shift two long gear levers simultaneously in different directions

around the 12 ratios swiftly enough so that the high-revving engine didn't drop off into a bottomless trough of insufficient torque.

The ever-so-slow expansion of the Crook & Willington fleet was not a reflection of the lack of heavy traffic but more a result of the tight constraints in the days of 'A', 'B', and 'C' operators' licensing. MPT 527 had been sold to Siddle Cooks at Consett to ensure the latest Foden had a licence, but in 1954 Joe Elliott bought three vehicles and their respective licences from BRS Pickfords with a view to expanding the fleet. Amongst them were two rust-buckets that would never run again but the third, DDW 89, did move a phenomenal amount of weight for the carrier.

It was a four-in-line low-loader similar to FUP 115, but

Wanting a six-wheeled articulated tractor unit which could also run in ballasted form, Joe Elliott turned to Foden to produce one of their famous specials. MPT 527, an FGTU 6/30 tractor unit, came to County Durham in August 1951. It had only a Gardner 6LW engine but with hand-operated reduction hubs driven through an eight-speed gearbox, the Foden – especially with later owners – was to move a phenomenal amount of weight. The vehicle is seen not long after delivery, taking on a 43RB machine at Cold Heselden in County Durham. The digger was used on building radar stations both here and at Seaton Carew before being transported down to Rotherham. The crew members visible are Arthur Baldwin, Bobby Evans and Tony Swan.

NUP 234 was Crook & Willington's second Foden six-wheeler. Chassis number 34508 was delivered to the haulier on May 13, 1953, and classified as an FGTU 8/80. The larger, eight-cylinder Gardner engine and a 12-speed epicyclic gearbox were fitted, with a power take-off rated for 80hp. As well as a standard 32-gallon fuel tank, the vehicle was also equipped with a 50-gallon tank to the rear of the cab. The resourcefulness of the haulier is illustrated in the way this crane girder from Palmers of Hebburn is being carried on a tank-transporting trailer. Driver Arthur Baldwin took this photograph of the vehicle on the Birtley by-pass, with the spoil heap at Washington F pit just visible in the background.

the big difference in this 1942 Scammell, which had started life with Robert Wynns, was that it had solid tyres both on the trailer axle and on the tractor drive axle. 50 tons was regularly thrown onto the Scammell's back, meaning axle loadings on those two axles were bound to be in the region of 35 tons. It thus wasn't surprising when this Scammell hit the headlines of the *Cleckheaton Evening Despatch* dated September 1, 1954, because it simply sank into the tarmac roadway up to its axle centres.

It was not simply a case of the company *wanting* to use vehicles like this faithful, tough old Scammell, it was because their efforts in front of the licensing authority to upgrade their vehicles rarely met with success, such was the scale of opposition mounted by other competing hauliers in general and British Railways and BRS (Pickfords) in particular. However after repeated attempts the authority eventually was convinced by arguments of common sense and Crook & Willington Carriers were allowed to put on the road their strongest vehicle yet.

Even now, more than 40 years since they were built, the old Diamond T tractor units still have an indefinable something about them. Both TUP 5 and VPT 85 were 1945 productions but, bought as new, 10 years later, they were soon painted up and made ready for work. Both came through the Ministry of Supply as ballasted tractors but when worked by C & W they were normally run as artics hauling tank transporting semi-trailers.

It may seem rather strange but in the middle 1950s, ten

Above: PPT 672 was delivered from Fodens on May 11, 1954, the haulier paying £4,149 12s 0d for the tractor unit plus an extra £5 as a delivery charge. Chassis number 36346 had the six-cylinder Foden two-stroke engine and a 12-speed gearbox. The 60hp power take-off drove a Garwood roping winch. The Foden is seen coupled via its heavy-duty SAE fifth-wheel coupling to a 25-ton cranked frame low-loader, fitted with Michelin Metallic tyres, that came new from Cranes of Dereham in June 1954. Tony Swan drove this tractor for 15 years; it was eventually sold for scrap for £200. Centre: it was a rare sight to see both of Crook & Willington's two Classic Fodens out together. This Arthur Baldwin photograph shows the two low-loaders en route to Birkenhead docks, their loads being built by Hunslet of Leeds and destined for export to India. Whilst Arthur's leading Foden is carrying the locomotive, weighing 40 to 50 tons, Tony Swan's vehicle is simply carrying the tender which was only about 25 tons in weight. The crew cabs on both these vehicles were built as standard on the tractors by Foden, unlike the additional crew area on MPT 527 which was constructed by the haulier. Right: as a way of increasing the fleet, Joe Elliott bought three vehicles from BRS (Pickfords) after denationalization. DDW 89 was one of this trio and it had originally started life in South Wales. It was used by Crook & Willington to carry loads up to 50 tons in weight. The vehicle is pictured in Watling Road, Bishop Auckland, the haulage operations of the company being run originally from a shed in the garden of number 5.

117

The arrival of the two Diamond Ts was to add an extra dimension to the work-load of Crook & Willington Carriers. Seen here on trade plates near the Percy Street workshops shortly after being painted in 1955 is one of the two American imports, subsequently registered TUP 5. As standard, the tractor had the six-cylinder Hercules diesel engine and was fitted with Michelin Metallic tyres. Of the two Diamond Ts, this vehicle was the one most often used in ballasted form.

years after the end of the Second World War, battle tanks were a regular cargo. Whilst old ones were taken from storage to be cut up for scrap, there was still a big export market which saw new tanks being taken to the docks for onward transportation. These mostly tended to weigh off in the 40 to 50-ton region, but there were exceptions. At 73 tons the Caernarvon was not only a lot heavier than the Centurion, it was bigger and its sheer size and overall dimensions made some people nervous about carrying it. Crook & Willington put outriggers on the side of their tank transporters to take the extra width but even then it was critical to set the load dead centre. From 41 AVD Burn near Selby to ROF Dalmuir, Glasgow, was a long haul for the Foden but apart from stopping at Newcastle to have the brakes adjusted up, the load was safely delivered.

Tony Swann contended that nothing would stop the Fodens provided you gave them time. It was calculated that on maximum revs of the two-stroke, in bottom gear and low-ratio hubs, the Foden would progress at a maximum of five-eighths of a mile per hour, which by my reckoning is 55 feet per minute. Not really hasty, but it gave the Foden the independence to tackle anything solo in the days when only the likes of the affluent Pickfords could afford to send double-heading tractors out as a matter of course. Everyone else did the best they could. Even Tony remembered needing the strangest of assistance one day.

Clawing up Beacon Hill on the A34 near Newbury, Tony felt the Foden wasn't going to make it. The problem was not lack of traction, but with the drive axles digging in so hard, the front, steering axle was simply lifting clear of the roadway. Although the road was straight the camber eased the Foden relentlessly towards the nearside ditch. It took the

Top: to increase the potential carrying capacity of their articulated low-loaders, Crook & Willington modified the neck and added on a set of axles to allow up to 80-ton loads to be carried on the 22ft-long loading well. VPT 85 was recalled as being quite a brisk machine and definitely the quicker of the two Ts. Its normal driver was Harry Maggs who made a point of keeping the vehicle in a very clean condition. The one way of distinguishing between the two Diamond Ts from the side was that only VPT 85 had a ventilation flap adjacent to the nearside door. Centre: Bobby Evans is pictured in TUP 5 whilst the vehicle is parked in Watling Road on the outskirts of Bishop Auckland. Tank transporting was how Crook & Willington firmly established themselves. The semi-trailer seemed a shade on the high side but the incline to the rear was regularly utilized by the C&W staff. The Garwood winch mounted behind the cab would drag the dead tanks onto the trailer, but unloading them was a lot quicker. Once the spring-loaded ramps were dropped back, the tank was held on a chock and the winch rope removed. Then knocking the chock clear saw the battle tank unleashed like a freshly launched battleship. Above: as a heavy haulage team the Crook & Willington quintet were second to none, so it was not surprising that the Sunter brothers were keen to co-opt them into their fleet in one fell swoop. This Ernie Johnson photograph was taken as part of the package put together to show the make-up of the fleet to the potential purchaser. As can be seen, all the six-wheeled articulated units were coupled to tank-transporting semi-trailers.

assistance of a local farm tractor, hooked onto the front bumper, to provide steering so that the Foden could be pointed in the right direction and the hill cleared.

The Diamond Ts were also moving their fair share of weights. By utilizing a standard tank transporter bogie in a conventional low-loader body, Crook & Willington produced a very strong trailer capable of 80-ton capacity. The one drawback to this construction was that with the bogie right at the rear its manoeuvrability was terrible, creating all sorts of routing difficulties. Joe Elliott (Junior), known as Sonny to the rest of the driving staff, was supervising Bobby Evans on the haul of an 80-ton 1201 Lima out of Spennymoor open-cast coal site one day when they found it impossible to take one particular turn. They had no option but to go in the other direction and the instructions that Sonny gave Bobby as they approached one bridge were to take it nice and easy, stay in bottom gear, don't jerk the transmission, but whatever you do don't stop. The Diamond T must have been grossing well over the 100-ton mark but in this smooth manner the crossing was completed without incident – even though the bridge did have a 5-ton limit on it.

Sonny Elliott did in fact take over the running of the company when his father died suddenly in 1956 at the age of 50. He was to make a good manager of the business but the confusing demands for death duties on the Elliott estate made the sale of the heavy haulage business inevitable. The Sunter Brothers of Northallerton were quick to snap it up as a going concern, the five low-loaders being kept running in their original yellow livery. They were also run out of their old depot for the first six months but then the garaging was moved to Browney Colliery near Meadowfield.

These arrangements couldn't last, for the separate identity of the two operations created all sorts of minor friction. The Crook & Willington men were used to being given more responsibility and allowed to make more of their own decisions, a big contrast to the Sunter men who were worked hard by the demanding brothers. It's not that the C & W men were lazy – in fact, moving battle tanks between Burn near Selby up to Birtley near Newcastle, the Crook & Willington men were doing a load a day whilst the Sunter men with conventional low-loaders were having to take two days for the same type of tank – it was more a matter of style and attitude. By the early 1960s the Meadowfield depot was closed and the fleet withdrawn to Northallerton and put more under the control of Tommy Sunter. The vehicles were eventually to disappear through the passage of time although their old staff still had some major contributions to make in the transport world.

Tony Swann, Jimmy 'Geno' Goulding and Jack Emms were to make their mark as leading Sunter drivers whilst Arthur Baldwin went overseas and was to end up as manager at Thorntons Heavy Haulage in Rhodesia. Sonny Elliott, a chartered civil engineer by trade, went back into civil engineering to form Elliott Earthmoving in 1963. He now runs Elliotts Motors, the well established Bishop Auckland Ford car dealership. All are fine representatives of a long-gone company with a worthy reputation.

```
Fleet List
CROOK & WILLINGTON CARRIERS LTD

Vehicles known to have been operated by this company

Reg no    Make and type                       Sold to
EPT 237   International four-wheeled tipper
LME 985   Austin four-wheeled tractor
FUP 115   Scammell 4x2 artic unit             Sunters
MPT 527   Foden 6x4 artic unit                Siddle Cook
NUP 234   Foden 6x4 artic unit                Sunters
PPT 672   Foden 6x4 artic unit                Sunters
DDW  89   Scammell 4x2 artic unit
GXC 547   Scammell 4x2 chain-drive unit
FGH 350   Foden 6x4 winch tractor
TUP   5   Diamond T 6x4 artic unit            Sunters
VPT  85   Diamond T 6x4 artic unit            Sunters
```

15: Arrow Bulk Carriers Ltd

As Crook & Willington Carriers were approaching their untimely end in the mid-1950s, another Classic Haulier from yesteryear was just in its infancy. In the highly specialized field of liquid haulage, Arrow Bulk Carriers Ltd of 50-52, Lime Street, Hull were to champion the highest standards that a road haulier could adopt in a fairly short operating history of less than 25 years.

Arrow Bulk as a company was formed in September 1954, although the reasons behind their setting up actually go back to 1947 and the difficult period following the Second World War. The Rubber Estates Agency, who were responsible for channeling demand for their products, decided to form International Bulk Liquids (Storage & Transport) Ltd, its purpose, as the name suggests, being to store and transport, in bulk, liquids which were moved on an international basis. There was a huge demand for natural latex, and at first it had to be transported from the Far East in 50-gallon drums. It is a particularly difficult product to carry in bulk but there was a breakthrough when it was realized that if ammonia was mixed with it, the latex stayed fluid and would not coagulate.

Transporting it halfway round the globe was put in the hands of deep-sea ships of the Ben Line and as a reception point IBL decided to set up static tanks at Hull. At this time Hull was a thriving port, perhaps in the country third only in importance behind London and Liverpool. It was John R. Stovell, the late Managing Director and Chairman of IBL who liaised with the late John Whittaker to form IBL's reception facilities. Whittaker was a local man and already operated tank barges round the port of Hull, so the two were able to work together to ensure that the natural latex could be easily handled once it arrived.

IBL became operational in late 1949, a period as far as road haulage was concerned which coincided with nationalization. Thus to deliver the newly imported latex, the liquid was poured into drums and placed on the back of British Road Services lorries. However, as the industrialized world gradually got back onto its feet, delivering latex by the drumful began to seem totally inefficient. Contact was made with the company of J.L. Townson who offered to contract two road tankers to IBL so that the latex could be delivered in loads of 2-3,000 gallons at a time, thus cutting out the time and waste in filling individual steel drums. Once the receiving customers had their own storage tanks installed, the tanker operation was ideal. It was not long before John Stovell felt that, such was the increasing demand for their products in bulk, IBL should form their own road tanker company.

The credit for the name Arrow used for this company goes to John Stovell's wife. 'Well,' she said, 'an arrow goes straight from one point to another with speed and efficiency. Why not call it Arrow Bulk?' The name seemed to have the right presence to it and the suggestion was immediately adopted. In practice, however, the early vehicles did not really live up to what was expected.

In 1954, the truck building business was in an enviable position. Every truck they made could have been sold to hundreds of customers. Waiting lists of between one and two years were the norm so as a matter of necessity Arrow were obliged to buy two second-hand tankers which had been ran by Townsons on contract to them. Towsons in turn had also bought them second-hand, although their one previous owner, Shell Mex-BP, had clocked up about 700,000 miles on each of these weathered Scammells before deciding to part with them.

But, age of the vehicles apart, Arrow was in business and by the following year their services were also in demand to move such diverse products as acid and bitumen, as well as their parent's own speciality, natural latex. July 16, 1956 was an important day for Arrow Bulk, for on that day Mr E.W. Tomlinson (Eddie) was appointed as Manager. He had already earned an enviable reputation for his skilful management of transport especially in the developing operations of Unilever Ltd and on his shoulders the reputation of Arrow was to develop and prosper for the next 21 years.

As an operational tool, Eddie Tomlinson was to opt for the Scammell-Thompson-Gardner combination whenever he could – as far as he was concerned, there was nothing could beat them. Arrow ran Scammells until well into the 1970s and it speaks volumes for their engineering that through the millions of miles they travelled for Arrow there were never any faults with a gearbox or differential. The Scammell products of this era were justly renowned, although you paid a premium in price well above a similar Leyland or AEC outfit. But once it reached your turn to collect your new vehicle from Watford, you were treated almost like royalty. An appointment was made, the vehicle fully examined and explained, a test drive was arranged; you weren't buying any old tanker, you were taking delivery of one of the best, a Scammell.

But Arrow, like everyone else, sometimes had to make do

with other permutations of vehicles, tanks and engines. Foden eight-legger MBU 14 is particularly remembered from that early period. An S18 FE6/24, it had as its designation suggests, the Foden-made Mark 2 two-stroke engine. Its crisp bark almost bit into the air as it drove along, with a top-speed capability recalled as being around 80 mph. It couldn't stand the pace it set for itself, though, and it even had to be returned to Foden to have a cracked chassis repaired.

If getting suitable vehicles was quite a problem, then obtaining the required carriers' licences to allow them to haul goods on the road was probably more difficult. Good sales technique from Comberhill Garages of Wakefield resulted in an interesting pair of Atkinson rigid eight-wheelers coming to Arrow. Nothing odd in their specification or in their cost of £8,000 apiece, but what the brand-new tankers brought – for the addition of a mere £2,000 a time – was a special 'A' licence, which even on its own could command such an asking price.

Those first two Atky eight-leggers had the slow,

Opposite: one of the first vehicles to be employed by Arrow Bulk Carriers on contract licence for the carriage of rubber latex was the six-wheeled AEC Mammoth Major, registration number KBU 960, of 1954 vintage, seen here manoeuvring in the premises of International Bulk Liquids at Hull. George Rossiter, IBL foreman, is the man giving directions; Managing Director of IBL was Tom Moxon who is seen in the white coat. This weighbridge was to be updated with the change in weight limits, being replaced by one of 40 tonnes capacity. The AEC had a carrying capacity of 2,750 gallons, its tank being manufactured in a material known as Colclad. Above, right: put into service in January 1956, the Gardner 6LW-powered Scammel MBU 13 was originally bought to work on the movement of acid produced by Marchon of Whitehaven. It was first painted in the colours of Marchon and also originally had a far smaller acid-carrying tank on its BTC four-in-line running gear. Because of the density of this acid and the rearward slope of the barrel, punctures were a regular occurrence on the hard-worked trailer tyres. The vehicle was taken off the Marchon contract and its trailer retanked as shown here for dedicated sulphite lye work. The product is a derivative from the process of pulping timber for paper and was imported from Finland to be used as a binding agent in the manufacture of furnace bricks. As it has to be carried at a high temperature, the tank barrel, manufactured by YEWCO of Bradford, incorporates lagging and steam-heating coils. Below, right: MBU 14, also put into service in January 1956, similarly began in the dark port-wine colours of Marchon Products, carrying acid. It too originally had a smaller acid-carrying tank and it is recalled that the Foden chassis didn't take kindly to the work and its cracking prompted reflitching work back at the Sandbach factory. The FE 6/24 was fitted with the Mark 2 two-stroke engine and when the vehicle was at full song climbing Dunmail Raise – between Grasmere and Keswick – the noise could be heard 20 miles away. When fitted with a different, 4,000-gallon capacity barrel, the Foden was used on another dedicated contract carrying paraffin wax from Llandarcy to Hull for the production of Osgerby's fire lighters. To prevent the wax solidifying, the tank was well insulated and fitted with provision for steam heating.

Opposite, above: the Easthaugh brothers – Jack and Alf – ran a fleet of about eight tankers mainly on products connected with the paint industry like linseed oil. They favoured four-wheeled Albions and RKH 565 was the largest vehicle they operated. The Albion Chieftain tractor unit, which dates from 1955, is here coupled to tank trailer number one which had an unladen weight of 3 tons 16 cwt and was supported on Carrimore running gear. Pictured in Pearsons Park, Hull, the Albion is remembered as being a vehicle that none of the Arrow drivers liked after Easthaughs had been incorporated into that concern. However, the carriers licensing system then in force did allow for the licence from this artic to be transferred to a more acceptable eight-wheeled rigid. Opposite, below: LHL 298, pictured in the IBL premises at Hull, was one of two identical eight-wheeled Atkinson 1786 vehicles – the other one being 2405 KH – that were bought with an additional premium required for the special A carriers licence that came with them. These were also the last two vehicles that were bought new with the Gardner 6LW engine, going into service in March 1958 not long before the announcement of the more powerful Gardner 6LX engine. The vehicle was fitted with a Darham Industries stainless steel tank; being divided into two compartments and equipped with pressure discharge meant the cargo was unloaded to the centre of the nearside rather than at the rear. Tanker followers will appreciate the fine lines of the Darham tank which included a specially constructed hose box down its length. More impartial observers may wonder at the reasoning behind Atkinsons' windscreen wiper layout. Top: there were to be many customers who required latex but couldn't take delivery of a full eight-wheeler load, so Arrow Bulk ran a number of smaller four-wheelers specifically to meet that demand. Eddie Tomlinson recalled buying this Albion Clydesdale chassis because, although still regarded as a premium vehicle, it was a lot cheaper than the preferred AEC Mercury. The gleaming tank belies the fact that it started life carrying acid on the back of Foden MBU 14. After being removed from that chassis, the tank was cut down and refurbished to carry a maximum of 1,600 gallons of latex. Driver of the Albion was George Kidd who was to achieve a 20-year safe driving record with the company and never exceeded the speed limit. George Rossitter is standing at the rear. Above: going into service during January and February 1963, the three Foden S21 eight-wheelers in the Arrow Bulk livery, to the right of this group, were bought specifically to meet a contract with Esso for the delivery of heavy fuel oil to the early warning station at Fylingdales on the North Yorkshire Moors. The vehicles were double-shifted, worked six days a week normally, and on the seventh if required, to keep the Mirrlees engines of the generators going. Only one mishap was recalled on the lengthy contract, when 4118 RH hit a patch of black ice at Lund, East Yorkshire in November 1964. The loaded vehicle turned onto its side but the fine construction of the Darham Industries tank prevented it from rupturing.

Eddie Tomlinson quickly became a convert to the reliable performance offered by the 150 Gardner engine whether it was fitted in Atkinson, Foden or Scammell chassis. The only trouble was that he wasn't the only operator who felt this way and an order for this type of vehicle could mean waiting 18 months or two years for delivery. Bought far more quickly were a trio of AEC Mammoth Major eight-wheelers, 451, 452 and 453 GKH. Acquired from Phillips of Sheffield, the AECs went into service during January 1964, having multi-purpose tanks made of stainless steel by Darham Industries. Powered by the 11.3-litre 185bhp engine, the eight-wheelers were recalled as particularly fast machines. They were generally used, because of their pace, on the paraffin wax traffic from Llandarcy back to Hull.

ponderous Gardner 6LW engine but the next one, WWF 346, was recalled as being the first Atky to be made with the larger Gardner 6LX giving 150bhp. Only 38bhp between the two engines, but it was to mean all the difference to Arrow when combined with Gardner reliability. The Atky was immediately put onto a severe, testing routine which saw it double-shifted to complete a round trip between London and Hull each 24 hours. The pattern revolved round the town of Stamford with one driver doing Stamford-Hull-Stamford, whilst the second driver did the Stamford-London-Stamford leg.

Another Gardner-powered Atkinson of the late 1950s was also well remembered, but in a less favourable vein, for a trick which only came to light after it had been involved in

a minor accident. The vehicle simply reversed into the garage door, not the most exciting of incidents, but when the driver swore that he had engaged a forward gear at the time of the mishap, people naturally gave him some very strange looks. The minor damage was easily repaired and nothing else was said until a few weeks later when Arrow's head mechanic had occasion to go and move the small Atkinson four-wheeled tanker across the yard. The mechanic said that he went to reverse but for some reason found the vehicle going forward.

The engine manufacturers Gardner were contacted and after considered deliberation they admitted that their 5LW engine could in fact be made to run backwards. Apparently it depended on how the crankshaft came to a halt when last

Orobis Ltd was a subsidiary of BP Chemicals, their speciality being the supply of additives that were incorporated into the developing range of lubricating oils for the motor industry. Although their head office was in London, their production outlet was at Saltend near Hull. Arrow were to have up to eight vehicles solely on work for Orobis, and the traffic took them all over the UK and also via the Southampton-Le Havre route to destinations on the Continent. Back loads on those occasions naturally included oil. The beautifully built oval-section tank behind this Gardner-powered Foden tractor is stepped down from the fifth wheel coupling and features a central pumped discharge.

126

It was slightly ironical that Doverstrand chose Arrow Bulk Carriers as the main distributor of their produce, because Doverstrand produced synthetic latex at the Stallingborough factory whilst Arrow had originally been formed to deliver natural latex on behalf of IBL and the strides made in synthetic production meant that the use of man-made latex was quickly outstripping that of the more expensive natural product. The first vehicle run in Doverstrand colours was ARH 217B, a Gardner 150-powered Scammell Highwayman artic, and Arrow were eventually to have eight vehicles on the contract. The fine print on this ERF tractor unit gives its unladen weight as 5 ton 6 cwt, the complete outfit weighing 11 tons 1 cwt empty.

used, and was also related to the engine's having five cylinders. Little could be done about this engine's quirk, but all Arrow drivers who jumped into the little Atky were henceforth aware of what to be prepared for.

Four-wheelers of a different kind were absorbed into the Arrow business when the company bought out the Hull-based company of Easthaugh Bros Ltd. Easthaughs ran about eight small Albions, all being rigid four-wheelers apart from one Chieftain artic. Buying smaller operations out as going concerns was the only assured way of increasing the number of carriers' licences you had. It was always heavy going at the licensing sessions when an approach was made for a brand new licence, especially if it was a coveted open 'A'. However one customer, Eddie Tomlinson recalls,

agreed to go to court and support the application for Arrow's increase in operating vehicles. The reason behind the application was to cater for the new business of Eddie's customer but as usual, the other companies that were queuing up to object to the increase made it clear that they had ample numbers of tankers available to carry this traffic without Arrow being granted any more. This tack horrified the customer. 'Listen, Mr Judge,' he said with considerable directness, 'this stuff belongs to me and if I say I want it delivering on an Arrow vehicle, then it will be delivered on one of theirs and nobody else's, no matter how many spare tankers they have free.' The application was granted.

Arrows fought hard for their customers, like many others, and it was their image above all that they were so keen to

To mark the marriage between Calor Transport and Arrow Bulk Carriers Ltd in 1977, Eddie Tomlinson arranged for these ERF and MAN tankers to stand still long enough to be photographed together. Arrow Bulk had long since shortened their lengthy trading name for impact to the single word 'ARROW' on their fleet of vehicles. Arrow had long been users of ERF and had only given them up in favour of MAN because supplies of new vehicles to their dealer, Ashgrove, were in such small numbers. The Arrow fleet number can be interpreted by removing the first digit; the remaining number, 97 in this case, denotes the 97th tanker to be operated by that company since it was formed.

maintain. To that end, all the driving staff had their accident records carefully scrutinized. In conjunction with ROSPA (Royal Society for the Prevention of Accidents), returns were made for the staff's safety ability; ROSPA would give you a tankard after achieving five consecutive safe years and Arrow added to that with a hefty cash bonus. Whether or not a driver was at fault for an accident was a matter which could at times be hotly debated. To prevent any allegations of bias against the company, a small tribunal was set up, involving two senior drivers and the local Road Safety Officer, who would pass judgement if the driver felt badly done by.

Condition of the vehicle was another matter which largely influenced image and, after Arrow had bought out Easthaugh Bros, they transferred all the painting of their fleet to Ashgrove Motor Engineers, who had been an offshoot of Easthaugh. The vehicles continued to be mainly Gardner engined, but when Ashgrove took over as an agency for the ERF products, Arrow naturally decided to opt away from Scammell, Atkinson and Foden to ERF units still specified of course with the Gardner engine, the power of which was now up to 180bhp from the 6LXB.

This pattern might have continued to be followed for a considerable time were it not for a set of developments which, when linked together, eventually changed the whole face of the fleet. With the demand for more and more power in artics that were now running at 32 tons gross, Gardner produced their famous 240bhp machine, the 8LXB. Eight cylinders produced a sound all of their own and gave the operator the power he was after – provided he could pay a hefty premium of about £2,500 for the privilege. Arrow for one weren't going to have this oppressive costing over their heads and opted for the Cummins engine in its place. This went nicely with ERF vehicles but what did make things go sour was that ERF would only supply Ashgrove with one new unit a month or 12 units a year as new stock. As Arrow were buying about eight of these each year as their normal fleet replacement programme, it meant that Ashgrove, wearing their ERF dealer's hat, were only permitted to sell four units a year to the list of clamouring customers.

No matter how many representations were made to ERF they wouldn't budge on this strict quota, so naturally when the European truck makers came on the scene in the early 1970s, the Ashgrove-Arrow concern gave them close attention. It was to be MAN who were to make the biggest impression and as they promised that any agent of theirs could have as many new trucks as they wanted, the business sense behind going German overwhelmed the patriotic but restrictive attitude of buying British. Soon it was MAN 16.232 sleeper-cab tractor units that were acclaimed as both driver and company favourites.

But it was the gradual recession in tanker haulage that was to prove the big stumbling block that neither Arrow or their MAN tractors or the loyal staff could do anything about. When you have a fleet of 50 vehicles yet only have work for 40 of them, then cuts have to be made. Whilst the parent International Bulk Liquids had stayed quietly in the background without interfering whilst Arrow's profits were soaring, the recession made them look carefully at the need for running road vehicles.

It is a matter of public record that Calor Transport bought Arrow Bulk Carriers Ltd as a going concern in 1977, with no redundancies being forced on any of the Arrow staff, one commitment agreed before the sale. The decision by IBL to sell their haulage arm meant that the proceeds could be ploughed back into more storage facilities. It serves perhaps as a reminder to all those ardent followers of the transport scene that road haulage is simply a service, a service that this country could not exist without, but, in the free market-place that existed before and exists after that short period of nationalization, also a service that is highly competitive.

Arrow Bulk was created to perform a particular service, the movement by road tanker of natural latex in bulk. It developed into a highly respected haulier carrying all sorts of liquids as diverse as the strongest acids and the blandest vegetable oil. The agreed marriage to Calor Transport which meant that its individual identity quickly disappeared was simply that destiny which all Classic Hauliers of yesteryear have had to endure.

Fleet List
ARROW BULK CARRIERS LTD

Vehicles known to have been operated by this company

Reg no	Make and type	Reg no	Make and type	Reg no	Make and type
KBU 690	AEC six-wheeled rigid	4119 RH	Foden eight-wheeled rigid	HRH 602D	Foden eight-wheeled rigid
LBU 99	AEC four-wheeled rigid	6223 RH	Scammell 4x2 artic unit	JRH 298E	Scammell 4x2 artic unit
MBU 13	Scammell 4x2 artic unit	6157 AT	Scammell 4x2 artic unit	KRH 151E	Foden 4x2 artic unit
MBU 14	Foden eight-wheeled rigid	6158 AT	AEC eight-wheeled rigid	KRH 152E	Scammell 4x2 artic unit
MBU 650	Scammell 4x2 artic unit	451 GKH	AEC eight-wheeled rigid	MRH 622F	Scammell 6x2 artic unit
RKH 565	Albion 4x2 artic unit	452 GKH	AEC eight-wheeled rigid	NKH 616F	ERF 4x2 artic unit
LHL 298	Atkinson eight-wheeled rigid	453 GKH	AEC eight-wheeled rigid	PKH 569G	ERF 4x2 artic unit
2405 KH	Atkinson eight-wheeled rigid	454 GKH	Foden eight-wheeled rigid	PKH 570G	ERF 4x2 artic unit
WWF 346	Atkinson eight-wheeled rigid	ARH 217B	Scammell 4x2 artic unit	RRH 604G	ERF 4x2 artic unit
4376 KH	Atkinson four-wheeled rigid	BRH 238B	Foden eight-wheeled rigid	EAT 501L	ERF 4x2 artic unit
7529 KH	Albion four-wheeled rigid	CRH 718C	Foden eight-wheeled rigid	ORH 119M	MAN 4x2 artic unit
4116 RH	Foden eight-wheeled rigid	EAT 342D	Foden eight-wheeled rigid	PAT 926M	MAN 4x2 artic unit
4117 RH	Foden eight-wheeled rigid	GKH 179D	Foden eight-wheeled rigid		
4118 RH	Foden eight-wheeled rigid	GRH 228D	Foden eight-wheeled rigid		